FROM THE SIDE OF THE DESK

A Practical Guide to Shortening Your Job Search

by Jay D. Fusaro
with Rosemary D. Fusaro

Networking
Interviewing
Creating your playbook
Sharing job leads
Negotiating
Onboarding
and a great deal more ...

Inspire On Purpose Publishing
Irving, Texas

From the Other Side of the Desk
A Practical Guide to Shortening Your Job Search

Inspire on Purpose Publishing

Irving, Texas

(888) 403-2727

http://inspireonpurpose.com

The Platform Publisher™

Printed in the United States of America

Library of Congress Control Number: 2015944944

ISBN-13: 978-1-941782-21-7

ACKNOWLEDGMENTS

This book would not have been possible without the help of several people. First and foremost is my wife Rosemary. Without her support, patience, feedback, and editing, *From the Other Side of the Desk: A Practical Guide to Shortening Your Job Search* would never have been published. A special thanks also goes to Sonia Lowery of Lee Hecht Harrison; Bob Snelling of Snelling and Snelling; Jim Ashworth; Michelle Morse and Rebecca Chown of Inspire on Purpose; and Billye Johnson, Karen Beckman, and Caitlin Taylor. Their expertise, guidance, and friendship helped me make the right decisions, encouraged me throughout the process, and provided the necessary foundation.

Jay Fusaro

TABLE OF CONTENTS

FOREWORD

There's No Shortcut to Success

Preparing for a successful job search is not an intuitive process. Often, people think that because they have experienced success in other aspects of life, they will automatically be proficient at interviewing for a job.

In fact, the opposite is true. We achieved past successes, most likely, because we committed time and effort to learning the skills necessary to do so. When a job is on the line, it's especially important to acquire and master new skills.

The first thing to understand as you embark on your search is that job offers can be hard to get. Conducting a successful search takes significant effort and perseverance, and you must be willing to learn or polish a variety of skills related to networking, interviewing, negotiating, and onboarding.

Some companies claim they can take the "work" out of this endeavor by writing your résumé, sending it out, and setting up appointments for you, but if you are ever approached by one of these businesses, be very, very wary.

Such offers should sound too good to be true *because they are*. The fact is, if you wish to shorten the time it typically takes to land a new job, you need to put the same effort into learning the skills this book teaches that you put into achieving every other success you enjoy.

What qualifies me to offer interviewing and job search advice? In brief:

- I am a certified public accountant and finance professional with twenty-nine years of business experience. I've worked with large public companies for most of my career, many of them Fortune 1000 companies. As a hiring manager, I have interviewed hundreds of candidates and hired dozens. I know what it takes to perform well on an interview. By the same token, I know why some candidates fail to receive offers.

- Managing large corporate professional teams worldwide gave me a passion for mentoring and developing teams and individuals. A marked reduction in employee turnover is just one of the significant benefits of the internal mentoring programs I implemented at several companies.

- I further tapped into my passion for interview coaching when I found myself in transition in 2010. After not having had to look for a job in more than seventeen years, I suddenly found myself seeking new employment as a result of a management change. I received a great deal of help throughout this process, learned a tremendous amount, and expediently found a new job. In an effort to give back, I began helping others land jobs.

- I enjoyed this so much that I earned a coaching certificate from the Learning Resources Network in partnership with Southern Methodist University in Dallas and then started my own company, Eureka Professional Services. In addition to offering career coaching to individual clients and working with them to develop and sharpen their interviewing skills, I also offer public speaking engagements and consulting on a group or company basis.

- To date, my client success rate averages 65% using the techniques set forth in this book, while my own personal interview success rate was 66%. (I went on three interviews that resulted in two offers using these techniques). Obviously, these numbers are well above the industry average of 25%. Meanwhile, many of my clients receive multiple job offers and compensation packages that are markedly higher than anticipated.

In response to my clients' many requests for a published version of my approach to preparing for and landing a new job, I sat down and wrote *From the Other Side of the Desk: A Practical Guide to Shortening Your Job Search*. In this text, I convey the essential skills, tools, and techniques required to successfully network, interview, negotiate, and onboard at a new company. The material in this book applies to those seeking a new or first career, those overcoming the trauma of a job loss, and those who fear leaving a job that no longer fits their needs.

From the Other Side of the Desk also offers a "new" tool — the playbook — and explains why it separates you from the competition and dramatically increases your chances of landing a job.

In addition, this book outlines the typical flow of interviews and provides suggestions on what to say (and not say) during the interview. It also explains why the primary key to an efficient and effective job search is understanding the perspective of the person who is hiring you.

Because the prep work is so essential to a good outcome, the first section of the book — Getting the Interview — is the weightiest, but each section is vital to your long-term success.

My experience tells me that the right frame of mind and extensive preparation are essential components of a successful job search. For this reason, I urge you to carefully read each chapter of this book, regardless of where you are in your job search process. As you do so, ask yourself two key questions:

1. Am I getting interviews?

2. Am I getting job offers?

Although these questions may seem obvious, give them some thought. If you are getting interviews but no offers, your focus needs to be on your interviewing skills. If the interviews are not coming, it very well may be that your networking, your cover letter, or your résumé are the problem. You will need to determine the issue and adjust your focus accordingly. When handled properly:

- Every four to five résumés sent out should result in an interview

- Every three to four interviews should result in an offer

This is true whether you are applying for a job you hope will be a springboard to a different opportunity or whether, in fact, you are applying for your dream job. Regardless of the position or field, the skills and techniques provided in this book will enable you to conduct an efficient job search while significantly reducing both your anxiety and the time it takes to land the opportunity you seek.

Now is the time to turn your prospects around and take that important first step toward your new job. The methods conveyed in *From the Other Side of the Desk* lead to a more effective and shorter search, so let's get started!

Jay Fusaro

PART I

Getting the Interview

If you're looking for a job, you're in good company.

Perhaps, like so many others, you've been laid off, fired, outsourced, downsized, or — one of my personal favorites — "right sized" due to an economic downturn, a new management team, a merger, an acquisition, or a corporate strategic shift.

Or perhaps you've just graduated from college, are recently discharged from the military, or are returning to the workforce after a hiatus.

Whatever the reason, the outcome is the same: you need a job.

Start your search now. It can be tempting to sit around procrastinating, processing, or even licking your wounds, but do not give in to that temptation. Minimize the amount of time you hang your head and allow yourself to feel bad. As sad as it is, I agree with Daryl "Razor" Reaugh, color analyst/commentator for the Dallas Stars, who once said, "Don't bother to tell anyone your problems. Twenty percent don't care, and the other eighty percent are glad you have them."

Get into a routine. Be disciplined. You're in charge of your search, or you should be, not your spouse, your headhunter, your mentor, your interview coach, or any other outplacement consultant or career services advisor. You are the CEO of your own company as well as the CIO, CFO, and head of marketing. The product is you, and the objective is to get an interview and then a job offer.

I received a great deal of advice and feedback regarding my job search, and if you're lucky, so will you. You need to sort through all the information coming your way and mindfully develop the skills and tools that will allow you to elevate yourself and stand out from the crowd.

If you're ready to learn more, read on.

CHAPTER ONE

Lay the Foundation

Laying a foundation is the basis of success, regardless of your goal. When it comes to finding a new
job, laying this foundation requires you to understand
certain basic facts and take specific critical steps that
can either increase your chances of success or cripple
them.

It's Not about You

As you begin the process of searching for a job, please
remember one key point: *the interview is not about you!*
It is all about the other person — the person conducting the interview — and how you, the job candidate,
can solve his or her problems.

Jobs are not usually created to fit the candidate. On the contrary, candidates are expected to fulfill the needs of the company. Perhaps the company is looking to hire because it's expanding, changing direction, or filling a vacancy. Whatever the reason, the company has a hiring need. You, the candidate, need to present yourself as the solution.

When I was interviewing candidates in my role as hiring manager, it always disheartened me to hear a candidate say something like, *"This is such a great opportunity for me because it ..."* and then conclude with one of the following options: (1) *"allows me to take the next step in my career,"* (2) *"provides an introduction into this industry,"* (3) *"gets me into this great company,"* or (4) *"allows me to work for a public company."*

Such responses demonstrate that candidates care primarily about what is important for them personally rather than about the needs of their employer. Meanwhile, these responses overlook the fact that interviewers could not care less why this is a good opportunity for you.

Once you, as the job candidate, accept that the interview is not about you, the dynamics of the interview discussion change considerably in your favor.

However, there is much ground to cover before devising a strategy to prepare for interviewing, so let's get started by laying a solid foundation.

Manage Your Perspective

One of the most important things to remember when you have lost or are looking for a job is to maintain a positive perspective. How you look at your situation is tremendously important to your ultimate success. If you have lost a job, it is natural to want to hide out and tell no one. Allowing yourself a small amount of time to grieve and to indulge in a bit of self-pity is healthy. After all, our jobs are an integral part of who we are. Strip them away, and we feel lost until we find a new path forward.

However, job loss happens to nearly everyone at one time or another, and in today's economic environment, it seems to be happening more and more frequently. Instead of considering yourself "unemployed," start thinking of yourself as "in transition." After all, you are in the process of transitioning from one job to your next opportunity.

More to the point, the word "unemployed" implies inertia while "in transition" implies activity. Altering your terminology will create a big shift in how you, and others, view your current situation. As is often said, action conquers fear. The sooner you start focusing on the future and taking steps to improve your situation, the sooner you will land your next job.

Get Started Immediately (but Don't Get Addicted)

Looking for your new job is itself a job. Plan when you are going to "work" on your search, and consider sticking to the traditional 9:00 to 5:00 routine. This puts your workday in sync with that of potential employers' and prepares you for when you do eventually land a job.

Structure your search by dividing your time into portions devoted to creating the tools you need to market yourself (this is covered in Chapters Two and Three) as well as networking, researching, practicing for interviews, and following up with necessary administrative tasks such as writing thank-you notes.

Be sure to schedule breaks away from the job search just as if you were in an office so that you remain fresh. In the 24/7 world we live in, this is difficult to do. I'm not suggesting that you never check your emails, texts, or other social media after 5:00 p.m.; just be careful not to get addicted.

I fell into this 24/7 pitfall during my search and became obsessed, as my wife can attest to. Although I landed a new job relatively quickly, partly because I worked on my search and stuck to a schedule, I caution you to avoid becoming a hamster on the endless wheel.

Prepare Your Family

If handled properly, a job search is a full-time job in and of itself. You need to prepare your spouse or significant other for the rigors of this search, particularly the time and emotional effort it will require. As a fringe benefit, spouses or significant others can provide valuable feedback, support, and assistance.

When I was in transition, I initially failed to involve my family, which caused unnecessary stress in my marriage. Case in point, when I was conducting part of my job search away from the house, I spontaneously stopped on my way home one evening to get a haircut and did not return home until a few moments before we were supposed to meet friends for dinner. My wife, understandably annoyed, uttered the now famous words, "What were you doing all day that kept you from getting your hair cut earlier?"

It was a mistake not to inform her of the demands of properly conducting my search. Obviously, being well groomed is a key component of the job hunt, but no doubt my haircut could have been arranged to avoid bumping up against our evening plans.

Cultivate Confidence

As I mentioned in the Foreword, job offers are hard to get, and the process of conducting a successful job search is equally difficult. This can play havoc with your self-confidence at a time when self-confidence is precisely what you need.

Learning to exude confidence during times of uncertainty takes practice. To cultivate and convey this confidence throughout your job search, you need two things: a positive attitude and intense preparation.

To convey a positive attitude, hold your head up, throw your shoulders back, make eye contact, and smile when you meet people, whether casually or through your formal search efforts. Start practicing this now, and it will eventually become a habit. People want to be around (and work with) those who are positive and upbeat, so give off positive energy and be careful not to drain the energy from others.

That said, I firmly believe the best way to cultivate confidence is through preparation. Think about a time you had to give a presentation, sit for an exam, or meet with an executive. How did you feel when you were prepared versus when you decided to wing it? I'm willing to bet that when you were prepared, you exuded confidence!

I teach seminars and give presentations to groups numbering anywhere from twenty-five to several hundred, and I am always very confident because I know exactly what I am going to say and when I am going to say it. On the other hand, if I were asked to speak about a topic I knew little about, my confidence would be near zero, and my audience would recognize this.

In my opinion, about 80% of what candidates say in an interview should be scripted and the other 20% ad libbed. However, most candidates take the opposite approach. This is primarily why the average interview success rate is only 25%. I also believe this is why so many candidates have such high anxiety and low self-confidence going into an interview.

Manage Your Online Persona

Before you start the actual work of scoring an interview and landing your next job, take the time to set yourself up for success by managing your persona, or the image you present to the world. In this day and age, your social media image begins and ends with the Internet.

Create a Business Email Address. Since much of your communication will take place via the Internet, creating your business email address is a high priority. Take the opportunity to create an email account that is professional. While you may currently have a great email name that reflects your sports team preference, your favorite hobby, or even your status as a parent, it may not be appropriate for your job search. Now is the time to create a separate email address that is solely for and about business. Use your first and last name for ease of recognition, and if you are required to have a number or character in your account name, avoid using your birth date or year or the year you graduated from high school or college. These offer too much irrelevant information and may create security problems for you later.

Use LinkedIn. If you are not currently on LinkedIn, register now! LinkedIn is a great resource for business communication and research. Yes, you should include your picture with your profile. This picture should be a professional bust shot from the shoulders up. LinkedIn is *not* Facebook, so the picture you use should not be a vacation picture or a picture of your boat, motorcycle, or car, nor should it include your spouse, children, or the family pet.

If you want to be taken seriously, this picture must be professional, which means a suit and tie or at minimum a collared shirt and suit jacket for men and similar attire for women.

You do not need to fill out your entire profile to get started, but you must at least fill out your latest job as well as your education history. In addition, pay attention to the following tips on how to effectively use LinkedIn:

- Finesse your headline until it's easy and compelling to read.

- Make sure your summary is accurate and that it reflects your specialties.

- Quantify your work experience by adding specific numbers (i.e., years of experience or number of people you managed).

- Upload examples of projects and other professional achievements or contributions, assuming such examples are neither inappropriate nor confidential.

- Update the skills section on an as-needed basis as your skills grow.

- Add any volunteer work or organizations you are involved with.

- Utilize the "Search" function to locate other people in your field.

- Personalize your invitation to connect; don't send the generic sentence "I'd like to add you to my professional network."

- Share relevant business articles and other links.

Check Facebook and Twitter. Potential employers will look at online media resources to get an idea of what their job candidates are doing with their time and skills. Go to the "Activity" section of your page and click on "View" to see what others are allowed to see. Either remove or block access to inappropriate pictures. Even simple photos of you with a drink in hand or goofing around with friends can be a turn-off for serious employers. Profanity, even if posted by a friend, can be a deal breaker. Ask yourself this question: after looking at your social media presence, would *you* hire you?

Google Yourself. Google your name and see what pops up, and do the same for other social media platforms like Yahoo, Pinterest, Instagram, and the like. You can be sure your future employer will be doing this. If there's anything in the public eye that can show you in a bad light, be prepared to address and explain it. You really do not want to be surprised by what is out there.

Consider a Personal Blog or Web Page. Personal blogs and web pages can be positive resources if you manage them well. If you're just starting a blog or web page, use it to your advantage, as it can show creativity, intelligence, and excellence. If you've had one for a while, review the content just as you did your Facebook posts to make sure nothing will embarrass you or reflect poorly on you.

Seek the Assistance You Need

Do not try to go it alone. Seek the help you need. When I suddenly found myself in transition after seventeen years of not having to look for a job or go on an interview, I felt lost. Through research, professional services, networking meetings, and the help of friends, I started to re-learn the skills I needed. I met with over ninety people during my search, and ultimately I found two mentors who provided me with invaluable insights. In addition, because my wardrobe was primarily business casual and my fashion sense nonexistent, I sought advice from a fashion consultant.

Resources are available to help in any and all areas of your job search. They include:

- Outplacement services

- Mentors

- Business coaches

- Interview coaches

- Career coaches

- Résumé writers

- Fashion consultants

- Alumni groups

- Religious organizations

- Networking groups

- Veteran associations

- Other members in your peer group who are also in transition

Some of these services may be out of your price range, but others are cost-effective or even free. Don't assume that something is too expensive until you do the research. Consider how much time you will spend out of work and what you would expect to make in a month's time. Then consider the cost of these resources. If any of these services enables you to land a position more quickly — even by several weeks or months — the payback could be significant. In my case, I landed my next opportunity in about half the average time for someone at my compensation level, which means the assistance I sought paid for itself a few times over.

Keep in mind that you must be open to being teachable and coachable for business and coaching engagements to work. You may not like everything you hear, but coaches use their insight and ideas to create a marketable product for potential employers, and that product is you.

If you cannot afford paid advice, seek out mentors. There are bound to be plenty of people in your network who would be glad to offer advice and feedback. Help is usually available simply by asking nicely and showing that you are serious.

One caveat: again, be very cautious about engaging with an organization that offers to "do it all" with respect to your job search. These are the firms that promise to interview you, write your résumé, package you up, and make introductions on your behalf, with your only responsibility being to show up for the interview. These firms tend to be very expensive, and they usually over-promise and under deliver. As I mention frequently throughout this book, there is only one person fully capable of managing your job search, and that person is you.

CHAPTER TWO

Craft the Essential Tools of the Trade

Entire books have been written on how to craft the perfect business card, write the ideal résumé, and create the irresistible cover letter. Rather than reinvent the wheel, I am going to present a very concise approach with examples I know to be successful from the perspective of a hiring manager. Later in this chapter, I will also introduce the concept of a biography (bio) and explain when to use it versus the résumé, since this format has worked so well for my clients and me. Finally, I will conclude this chapter with the indispensable thank-you note. But first things first, and the very first thing you need to do well is introduce yourself.

Your Personal Introduction

Now is the time to prepare your personal introduction. This introduction is commonly called the "elevator speech" and is typically introduced with the words, "Tell me about yourself."

Please know that the person asking you to "tell me about yourself" is not actually interested in your life history or accomplishments or how great you are. This individual really just wants to know if you can answer a simple question succinctly. You should be able to communicate in approximately forty-five seconds enough information to answer this request. The fact is, if the person wants more information, they will ask follow-up questions.

When I was a hiring manager conducting interviews, if the candidate could not concisely answer the question "Why don't you tell me about yourself?", the interview was basically over. I assumed that applicants who were unable to answer this basic interview question would also be unable to describe their response to a complex situation in a concise manner, either to me, the hiring manager, or to other potential future colleagues.

Most people start their elevator speeches with what they do. For example, "I'm an accountant," "I'm a lawyer," "I'm a teacher," or "I'm a computer engineer." Keep in mind that while these descriptions may be accurate, they create a situation whereby you are likely to be pigeonholed solely on the basis of your job title.

I believe there are two much more effective and informative approaches to addressing, "Tell me about yourself." You decide which you are more comfortable with.

The first approach begins with a description of what you do followed by highlights of your most recent position and a brief description of what you want to do in your next opportunity. It is ideal for introducing yourself to networking contacts.

To craft this effective description of what you do, turn to an invaluable source of information, job descriptions themselves. Companies spend a significant amount of time and money developing these descriptions, and you should use them to your advantage. After all, whether you are talking about what you have done or what you want to do next, searching for the right phrase in the heat of the moment can be frustrating, time consuming, and detrimental to your success. Don't reinvent the wheel. Defer to job descriptions.

When you read a description that excites you, nab some of the phraseology to use in both your verbal and written presentation of yourself. For example, you might describe yourself as "detail oriented" or "collaborative" after reading that these traits are desired in applicants applying for a particular job.

When I was crafting my introduction, I "borrowed" various words and phrases and came up with this:

> *I am a CPA with a deep financial planning background. I have been very successful at leading and motivating teams on complex projects. I am also a difference maker who gets the job done and a creative problem solver and leader who sets high standards. I have both IPO and M&A experience, and most recently, I was head of Corporate Planning with a publicly traded $3B company. I am seeking a position where I can lead the company's overall financial planning, forecasting, and performance management process and provide the CFO with visibility and predictability in earnings in order to*

elevate the quality of information presented to both senior management and Wall Street.

Yes, that's a mouthful, but I practiced it so that it sounded natural. It contained all the professional information and action items I wanted my audience to hear, and I was able to deliver it in about forty-five seconds, which is optimal for a personal introduction.

This is a more intriguing way to present yourself than the humdrum, *"I'm a senior manager."* It breaks through the narrow confines of a pigeonholing title and invites the listener to ask for more information.

The second approach to introducing yourself effectively is to keep your elevator speech short, concise, and high-level. I prefer this approach for interviews, but this is a personal decision. You decide what works best for you.

When taking this second approach, break your introduction into three ten- to fifteen-second segments. The first segment should be about the early years of your professional career. The middle segment will cover your last position, or "what I did most recently." The final segment details what you are looking for in your next opportunity, which should just so happen to tie into the job description of the position you are interviewing for.

An example of this second approach goes like this:

I grew up in New Jersey through high school and attended college in Boston at Northeastern University. I relocated to Dallas in 1991. I have my CPA and most recently have been very successful at leading and motivating teams on complex projects. I have both IPO and M&A experience, and I was head of Corporate Planning for a publicly traded $3B company. I am seeking a position where I can lead the company's overall financial planning, forecasting, and performance management process and also provide the CFO with visibility and predictability in earnings in order to elevate the quality of information presented to both senior management and Wall Street.

This second approach is meant to be short and sweet. During an interview, keep in mind why the interviewer is asking this question and what the objective is. Again, it's to see if you can answer a simple question *concisely.*

Whichever approach you take, since your introduction is short, it will be easy to memorize. However, be careful that it doesn't sound memorized. Practice it often to create a natural sounding response, and make sure you do not rush to get through it. You might even consider recording your introduction to listen to and critique. No matter how great your speech is, it will not make a positive impact if you do not enunciate clearly and crisply. Remember, you may deliver this introduction fifty or a hundred times, but the other person will hear it only once, so deliver it with a smile and keep it fresh.

Business Cards

Handing out business cards may seem like a step back in time, but they are imperative when looking for a job because they allow you to appear professional and prepared when people ask for your contact information. Simply put, you do not want to be scribbling out your information during a critical introduction or other opportune moment.

Invest in a set of professional business cards, but keep them simple. Include only your name, professional credentials such as CPA or CFA, your cell phone number, your email address, and your desired industry or the job title you are seeking (i.e., Finance Professional). If you have an MBA, remember that this is a degree, not a title, which means it should go on your résumé, not your business card.

Cover Letters

Every time you mail or email your résumé to a networking contact or prospective employer, it should be accompanied (and introduced) by a cover letter.

Do not let your cover letter say more than it should about you. Keep it simple, honest, and clear about who you are and what you bring to the table. In other words, do not bloviate.

blo·vi·ate: \ˈblō-vē-ˌāt\ intransitive verb

blo·vi·at·ed, blo·vi·at·ing

Definition according to Merriam-Webster: to speak or write verbosely and windily.

Now is the time to think like a hiring manager. Hiring managers want to know what a potential candidate (you) can do for their company, but they typically do not have time to review in detail every cover letter that comes across their desks. They have one goal — to fill a position. Your cover letter needs to quickly and concisely communicate who you are in terms of what they need. If you can accomplish this, you are well on your way to getting an interview.

When I was in charge of hiring candidates, I spent very little time reading cover letters, and I was not impressed when applicants repeated the contents of their résumé in their cover letter.

If you want your cover letter to be noticed, make it short and to the point. One of my mentors, Jim Ashworth, taught me this format and I believe it is very effective. The cover letter needs to be crafted to catch the attention of the reader with content, not fluff. To achieve this, make sure your cover letter contains the following three very short paragraphs:

First paragraph: *"I am responding to your ad in* [mention the outlet or company website] *for the position of* [name the position]." Then briefly describe two to three skill requirements of the position that you possess. Use relevant information from the job description that addresses these skills.

Second paragraph: *"When you read my summary of qualifications* [make sure this material ties your cover letter to your résumé], *you will see that I meet the requirements of the position and that I have the knowledge and skills to make a significant contribution to your team."*

Third paragraph: *"I look forward to an interview with your company."*

To see a full example of a cover letter I used when looking for a job, see the Exhibits section at the back of this book.

Résumés

The résumé is a business tool primarily used to impress a potential interviewer and get the interview; it is often used again in the actual interview. Although the résumé is accompanied by a cover letter when it is mailed or emailed, a cover letter is not necessary when the meeting is in person. In such instances, you will verbally introduce your résumé.

Essentially, the résumé comprises what are supposed to be your best and most meaningful professional experiences. While it is perfectly acceptable to source professional help in crafting and perfecting this tool, you must be able to own, defend, and communicate its contents. This is best accomplished when you write your résumé yourself.

Every four to five résumés you send out (about 20%) should result in an interview, and every three to four interviews (about 25%) should result in an offer.

If the interviews are not coming, one of two things is happening. Either you are not applying for the positions you are qualified for, or your résumé or cover letter is interfering with your results.

Check to see that your résumé meets standard expectations regarding length, style, and content. In a nutshell, résumés should be very brief on early history and should not:

- Exceed one page if you are currently in school or a recent graduate

- Exceed two pages unless you are in a technical field or have numerous publications or other extenuating circumstances

While it is tempting to include everything you have ever done professionally on your résumé, the reality is that only *recent* information is going to get you noticed. By focusing on your accomplishments from recent years and not those that span your entire career, you have a better chance of being noticed by the right people. Today, most job postings attract huge numbers of résumés, so a cursory glance may be all yours will receive. Make it count.

A copy of my résumé appears at the back of the book in the Exhibits section. Please refer to it as needed when crafting your own résumé and when checking out the style recommendations suggested here.

Introduction. At the very top of the résumé, state your name, including any professional titles (CPA, Ph.D., Dr., and so on), and your contact information. This includes your phone number, professional title or titles, and professional email address. Your home (street) address is not necessary.

Again, if you have an MBA, do *not* include it with your name because it is a degree, not a title. Many people make this mistake and include this degree on their business cards as well. While earning an MBA is admirable, it is unprofessional and pretentious to include it with your name. It belongs in the educational portion of your résumé.

Summary of Qualifications. A professional résumé should include up to fifteen bullet points that summarize your qualifications. If you are a recent graduate, include no more than nine bullet points. Bullet points can easily be arranged to fit the specific job requirements for the position you are applying for. Take advantage of this, as it allows you to customize your material and present yourself more like a "perfect fit."

Carefully read the job requirements of the position you are applying for. Assuming you possess these competencies, mirror these words in your summary of qualifications.

If you are a recent graduate, do not forget to include the competencies you gained through your experiences with internships, charitable functions, extracurricular campus groups, or as a volunteer.

Write a brief, four- to five-sentence summary of your qualifications immediately following the bullet points. Use real examples from your background in this summary, and once again, make sure it mirrors the requirements of the position you are applying for.

Professional Experience. Traditional résumés are usually set up in reverse chronological order with the most recent experience listed first. Be sure to include a brief description of each of the companies that employed you.

Other Important Considerations

There are other important factors to keep in mind when creating a résumé. Doing so will set you apart from the competition and make it a more likely that you advance in your job search.

Be ready to address the "So what?" factor. For every bullet point you include, you need to be able to effectively answer the "So what?" question, or why this point matters. The easiest way to accomplish this is to prepare a few sentences that illustrate or illuminate that point, following the "SAR" format of Situation, Action, Result.

To craft these sentences, break down each bullet point into the following parts:

- A description of the situation or problem you experienced

- What alternatives you considered and what action you took (including your role in that action) in order to resolve the issue

- The result of this action

I talk about this more later, but for each bullet point on your résumé, you also need to prepare a short story of about twenty-five to forty seconds that further illustrates or illuminates that point. You can use the SAR approach to develop these short stories, too. As I discuss in Chapter Three, these will come in handy when you are asked to give examples of specific points from your résumé.

When writing your bullet points, start with a descriptive adjective such as "developed," "established," "built," "hired," "trained," "reduced," or "increased." Then, as support, include phrases such as "resulted in…[lower costs, higher margins, increased profitability and/or production]," "which led to… [lower costs, higher margins, increased profitability, production]."

You get the picture. State your role (action), then the result (outcome of your action).

Quantify your accomplishments. Wherever possible, use specific numbers, dollars, and percentages. The fact is, in a results-oriented environment, you must be able to state a measurement of your accomplishments. Did you contribute to productivity improvement, reduced downtime, increased cost savings, or other identifiable measurements? How did the new program benefit the bottom line?

Keep in mind that if you either do not know or do not remember the exact amount, you can use words such as "about," "approximately," "more than," or "less than." However, you must always be as truthful as possible about the actual events that took place.

Résumé "don'ts." Finally, keep in mind some important things *not* to do in your résumé:

- Do not use phrases such as "professional with over twenty-five years of experience." While you should be proud of your many years of experience, do not let the number of years become the focus. Instead, stress the range of your experience and emphasize the elements that are pertinent to the position you are seeking.

- Do not use the word "executive." Instead, use "professional." Prior to the recession of 2008, "executive" was the acceptable term, but like most buzzwords, it went out of fashion. Do not date your résumé with old or over-used verbiage.

- At the risk of repeating myself, do not use "MBA" as a title. Instead, include this degree in the education portion of your résumé along with your BA or BS and any other degrees.

- Do not package your résumé in a special folder or binder with letters of recommendation or samples of your work. Unless you have specifically been asked to include these, save them for the interview.

- Do not include the month in the dates you worked for a company. Rather than "March 2010– December 2012," simply use "2010–2012." Some job applications do require months, but it is not necessary to include them on your résumé. It just adds unnecessary clutter.

Not all companies will respond to your cover letter and résumé, especially if your communication is poorly written or if you are answering a blind job ad. Nonetheless, the first impression you make on the hiring authority will often be through your résumé, so think of it as your interview suit on paper. How you present yourself through this document can make the difference in receiving a call for an interview or being forced to conclude that your résumé ended up in the recycling bin.

The All-Important Bio

During the job search process, it is very important to have all the necessary tools and to know when to use each one. In other words, sometimes the best résumé is not a résumé at all.

Enter the bio, a quick, one-page summary of you as a person as well as an employee. Unlike the classic résumé, the bio is a narrative of your work history with associated information about your professional training, accomplishments, and a smattering of business philosophy. Think of it as an extended written version of your forty-five-second response to the request, "Tell me about yourself."

In my opinion, leading with the bio is often more effective than leading with a résumé during a networking meeting. Because the bio combines aspects of the résumé with a marketing plan, it results in a user-friendly document you can incorporate into your job search, especially when mingling with business associates in your network. Simply put, the bio provides a softer sell than the résumé and is typically used when networking, whereas the résumé is primarily used to get the interview and for reference during the interview.

Two things typically happen in networking situations when you hand someone your résumé. First, the résumé tends to scream, "Find me a job!" This can be off-putting and does not allow the person to get to know you or take advantage of the true objective of the networking meeting. Second, when handed a résumé, people typically begin critiquing it and making suggestions regarding content or style. For these reasons, when networking, a bio is often more appropriate and more functional. It does not replace your résumé, nor does it entail crafting a detailed history of your entire life; it simply incorporates much of the information that is on your résumé into an easy-to-read, one-page networking tool.

Keep in mind that most people really do want to help you. Your job is to help them help you, and giving them a bio to start off with is how you accomplish that goal. After all, it includes those attributes and competencies you bring to the table as well as pertinent information about companies and industries you are interested in pursuing.

As with your résumé, be prepared to answer questions based on your bio by crafting short stories of twenty-five to forty seconds about the various pieces of information you include in your bio (i.e., your experience, qualifications, and other business details).

A copy of my bio is included in the Exhibits section at the back of this book. As with the cover letter and résumé, please refer to it when creating your bio. In the meantime, here are a few specific tips to start you off:

Cut and Paste Your Competencies. The bullet points on your résumé listed under "Summary of Qualifications" can be used under "Competencies" on the bio. Just cut and paste them from your résumé.

Include a Professional Picture. I am a strong believer in including a photo on your bio. The photo should convey an image that is both casual enough for this type of marketing tool and businesslike enough to present a professional image. It is well worth the money to hire a professional photographer to take this photo. This is not a requirement, of course, but it does help other networkers remember who you are. As the old adage says, "A picture is worth a thousand words."

Some might ask, "If I'm not putting my picture on my résumé, why put it on my bio?" The simple answer is that the picture further communicates to others that your bio is *not* a résumé. Instead, it is a networking tool, one that my own experience and that of my clients tells me is very well received.

I want to emphasize that creating a bio does not mean that you abandon your résumé. They are separate business tools, and both should remain part of your working toolkit. Wherever you take your bio, make sure you have your formal résumé with you just in case you are asked for one. Who knows ... As happened for me on one memorable occasion when I was in transition, the networking meeting could turn into an interview! Plus, some people simply prefer to see a traditional résumé or they may want one to pass on to a potential lead.

Create a Target Company List. An important aspect of the bio is that it lists the companies you want to target in your job search. This list answers the big question you will be asked by the person you are networking with: "How can I help you?" Regardless of whether or not you decide to develop your own formal bio for distribution, it is critical that you think about and put together a target company list. When you share this information, it makes it easier for other people to help you focus on your goals and identify contacts within the companies you are most interested in approaching.

Your list should include ten to twelve companies at most. These should be a mix of private and public companies, unless your vocation dictates one over the other. You can source companies in your local markets through the *Book of Lists* published by The Business Journals. This handy reference tool lists local companies by size, revenue, industry, and whether they are publicly or privately held. As mentioned earlier, another great source for company connections is LinkedIn.

Put another way, your target list gives people the opportunity to help you in your job search without putting them on the spot by asking them to find you a job. As I discuss in Chapter Four, an important goal of networking is to make it easier for the person with whom you are networking to help you. The bio does this by sharing your objectives with the other person.

Developing your target list should take several hours (not days!) of hard research, and it will change as your job search evolves. As your market knowledge grows, this list can be further refined.

If appropriate, I strongly recommend that you include the company of the person with whom you are networking on your target list. Excluding this company could be considered a glaring omission and disrespectful to the person who is taking the time to network with you. The exception to this is if you have neither the interest nor the skills or qualifications required to work with this company. In any event, you should be able to explain your reasoning if asked.

Thank-You Notes

In today's fast-paced environment, thank-you notes are less about handwritten notes on monogrammed vellum paper and more about promptly expressing your heartfelt gratitude. A handwritten note is nice if you are so inclined, but today, thank-you notes are usually sent via email.

Either way, in addition to extending your gratitude, the thank-you note is a way to remind, recap, and make a positive second impression. A good thank-you note might not change the mind of a networking contact who has already decided you are not the best fit for a position, but in a competitive situation, failing to send a thank-you note can eliminate you.

Thank-you notes should be sent to each person with whom you network or interview as well as to any others who help you land a meeting or interview.

Specifics of Crafting the Thank-You Note

First and foremost, include the name of the person you met and check and double-check the spelling. If you are using a program with auto-correct, make sure it has not "helped" you by altering a perfectly good name. To paraphrase the famous quote, "I don't care what you say about me as long as you spell my name correctly."

In addition, a good thank-you note or email should adhere to the following guidelines:

- In your opening sentence, include the circumstances, date, and time of the meeting. For example, *"Thank you for meeting with me Thursday morning at ABC Corporation regarding the position of assistant director of research."* The same holds true for phone interviews. Supply some information to jog the memory of the busy person who met with you.

- If your meeting was an interview, let the hiring authority know you will be happy to answer any additional questions that may arise.

- If you were networking and your host offered to make introductions, remind her of that in the next paragraph and thank her in advance for this offer. Also, remember to send a note at a later date *after* you've met with these contacts.

- If the meeting was an interview, end with something simple such as, *"I am confident that with my background and experience, I can make a significant contribution to your team. I am very excited about the opportunity to move forward in the process. Thank you again."*

- Close with a simple "Sincerely," "Yours truly," or "Best regards."

- Send your thank-you note or email within twenty-four hours of the interview or networking meeting. After all, some companies make decisions within that twenty-four-hour period.

If your note is written by hand and mailed, include a business card. You obviously cannot include a business card in an email, but you can easily make your email signature into something resembling an electronic business card that contains all your contact information.

With these basic tools of the trade carefully crafted and in hand, you are well on your way to landing the job you desire.

CHAPTER THREE

Create Your Playbook

Assuming your skills and training are valid, the way you separate yourself from the competition is through your preparation. You do this first and foremost with the help of an important and underutilized tool I call the playbook.

A New Tool for a New Age

Every sports team has a playbook that provides options, ideas, and approaches for the best way to handle any situation that may arise on the field or court. Whether you are in transition or seeking a better opportunity, a playbook is a vital resource to help gather thoughts and ideas and keep you focused on your objective — getting the job you want as soon as possible.

Picture a pyramid such as my company logo that appears on the back cover of this book. Most of your competition is at the base of the pyramid. These are the people who haphazardly send out résumés for any job that interests them. If they manage to get an interview, many of them "shoot from the hip" and ad lib their way through it. Your goal is to move to the top of the pyramid and be among the select few who perform at a high level in the interview. This takes effort, and developing your playbook is a key step in the process.

Part of the reason my clients' success rates are well over twice the industry average is that they are adequately prepared; developing a playbook is an integral part of that preparation. It may sound over-whelming, but virtually everything you are going to say in a networking meeting or interview should be scripted in this playbook. Thorough preparation for any possible situation and question you may face will minimize verbal missteps and give you much greater confidence. Essentially, this approach allows you to come up with your best answers while you are in a no-pressure situation.

Look at it this way: since you know your own background, can research the individual you will be meeting with, and can determine the basic questions you will be asked, very little of what you say in a networking meeting or an interview *should* be ad libbed. Yes, it takes time and effort to put this playbook together, but you only have to prepare it once. After that, it simply grows and evolves as you add new information.

Before I developed the playbook concept, I found myself preparing anew for each interview. At the same time, I noticed that certain questions were asked over and over. Once I began keeping all this information in one place, it became easier to rehearse and remember without constant practice. This gave me more time to review position-specific information before going on an interview. Developing my playbook actually reduced my overall workload, even though it ended up being more than twelve pages long!

Keep in mind that when you are interviewing, the interviewer is well prepared. This person has reviewed your résumé, looked up your LinkedIn profile, knows (and perhaps designed) the job description, is familiar with the company, and most likely has prepared questions in advance. To do well, you need to be equally prepared.

Five Critical Elements

Your playbook should contain the following elements:

1. Your forty-five-second personal introduction

2. A list of personal accomplishments with accompanying stories

3. Personal strengths and areas of improvement (i.e., weaknesses) with accompanying stories

4. Answers to fundamental networking and interview questions

5. Questions you want to ask (as well as questions you should *not* ask)

Forty-Five-Second Personal Introduction

As discussed in Chapter Two, this introduction, also known as "Tell me about yourself," is a quick overview of who you are and what you want to do. Craft it to give just enough information so that the listener will want to know more about you. Since every encounter is an opportunity to meet a workable contact or potential employer, a brief, well-honed introduction is an integral part of your playbook. Think of this intro as an abbreviated version of your résumé and keep it simple.

Personal Accomplishments with Accompanying Stories

Remember that you are both the salesperson and the product you are selling. To that end, develop a "laundry list" of ten to twelve items taken from the bullet points on your résumé under the Summary of Qualifications section that you can use when networking or interviewing. Then take this list and develop short twenty-five- to forty-second stories on each item that will allow you to provide greater detail when asked to do so.

As was the case when developing your bullet points in the résumé, start with descriptive adjectives such as "developed," "established," "built," "hired," "trained," "reduced," or "increased." Then, as support, select phrases such as "resulted in ... [lower costs, higher margins, increased profitability and/or production]" and "which led to ... [lower costs, higher, margins, increased profitability, production]."

Each story should inherently answer the question "So what?" The easiest way to accomplish this is to use the "SAR" (Situation, Action, and Result) format introduced in Chapter Two. For each bullet point, focus on a description of the situation or problem you experienced and the alternatives you considered to solve it, what action you took (including your role in that action) to resolve it, and the result of this action. For example:

(Situation) *The situation we were faced with was that the company could only forecast on a quarterly basis, and management wanted a forecast more frequently.*

(Action) *I assembled a cross functional team of both financial and systems experts within the company to develop a strategy and a project plan to meet management's goal.*

(Result) *After six weeks, we had a fleshed-out plan, and in seven months we implemented a twelve-month rolling forecast that we revised on a monthly basis.*

As mentioned earlier, quantify your accomplishments with specific numbers, dollars, and percentages.

In a results-oriented environment, you must be able to state a measurement of your accomplishments. Did you contribute to productivity improvement, reduced downtime, increased cost savings, or other identifiable measurements? How did the new program benefit the bottom line?

Using the same "SAR" formula with the "Strengths and Areas of Improvement" section below will allow you to be more concise and more effective in your delivery.

Personal Strengths and Areas of Improvement with Accompanying Stories

Come up with three strengths and one area of improvement (weakness) that you can confidently and comfortably discuss. Write these out in your playbook. Again, keep your answers short (only twenty to thirty seconds each), just as you did with the accomplishments. It is often helpful to bring in third party validation when possible, such as:

- *"My boss often recognized me for* [fill in the blank]."

- *"My supervisor consistently mentioned that I* [fill in the blank]."

- *"I've always been recognized as a* [fill in the blank]."

- *"I've been recruited by other departments to* [fill in the blank]."

- *"My 360 feedbacks have consistently noted that I* [fill in the blank]."

Such validation lends credibility to your strengths. Of course, it is essential that the third party you reference will corroborate your assertion if asked.

Again, always have a short story ready to back up the strengths you mention. When candidates tell me their strengths, I typically respond with, "That is very interesting; tell me more about the second one you mentioned."

This is often followed by either an awkward pause or a rambling, nonsensical answer, at which point it becomes clear that the candidate is unprepared and is trying to bluff his way through the interview.

That said, when addressing your weakness or area of improvement, choose judiciously. Your response needs to be legitimate and self-reflective but *never fatal to your ability to do the job you are applying for*. For example, when I was asked for my greatest weakness in an interview, I admitted that it lay in the area of technical accounting. This weakness was not fatal for me because, although I am a CPA, I was not pursuing a position that required a high degree of technical accounting expertise.

Answers to Fundamental Networking and Interview Questions

Every question and *every* answer you believe will be asked during a networking meeting or an interview should go in your playbook. In addition, every time you think of a new question or anytime you are asked a question you have not already prepared for, both the question and your answer should go in your playbook.

Basic questions you will be asked in either networking meetings or interviews or possibly both include the following (in the final section of the book, I provide additional common sample questions):

- Tell me about yourself.

- Walk me through your résumé.

- What are you looking for? (Networking only)

- How can I help you? (Networking only)

- Why should I hire you?

- Why are you interested in this company?

- What do you know about our company?

- What skills do you bring to the table?

- What are your strengths and weaknesses?

You should be able to address these fundamental questions clearly and succinctly, without much effort.

Questions You Want to Ask

The information you gather as part of your due diligence will also help you formulate questions you can ask and allow you to demonstrate that you have done your homework on the company. Prepare at least three talking points based on the information you have gathered. Typically, a candidate will only have the time to raise one to three key points, but asking smart questions can set you apart from the competition.

Questions can range from the very specific to the more general. Examples include the following:

- I've noticed that the company recently expanded into a new market in Houston. How is the rollout working?

- What are the most important attributes you see in the person in this position?

- What type of leader does the group/company need in this position?

- How would you assess the quality of the staff in the group?

- What are the two to three things keeping you up at night?

- Who is the ideal candidate for this position?

- Why do you enjoy working here?

- Why is this position open?

- Do you use 360 feedback?

- What would you like to see done differently by the new person in this position?

- Is there a team in place, or will I be putting the team together?

Questions you should not ask: As discussed above, you should come prepared with at least three relevant questions about the company, its products, growth plans, or the position itself.

However, when considering what to discuss, do not ask any questions that are controversial or contentious regarding the company, the interviewer, or the position. For example, do not ask about pending lawsuits or potential or recent layoffs. You are not an investigative reporter, and the company representative will not legally be able to discuss these issues. You are there to get an offer, not ask inappropriate questions. It is your responsibility to thoroughly research the company and determine if it is a viable prospect with a suitable company culture.

Also, do not ever ask either of the following questions during the initial stages of interviewing:

1. How much vacation time do I get?

2. What does the benefits package include?

These types of questions communicate to the interviewer that you are more interested in the perks of the job than in the job itself. This impression will eliminate you from serious consideration for the position.

Incorporate Due Diligence

Incorporate any and all research you do into your playbook. As interview appointments begin to be lined up, you will have individuals and organizations to research. Write everything down in your playbook.

Check out company websites, read recent press releases, and investigate as many resources as possible. If a company is publicly traded, look up the annual and interim reports as well as the analyst reports and listen to the most recent earnings call. All of this information can be found on the investor relations section of the company's website. Research any portion of the website that is applicable to the position you are interviewing for. Your ability to demonstrate your familiarity with the company you are interviewing with will show that you made the extra effort, and this effort will pay off.

Often, an interviewer will open with "What do you know about our company?" You need to be prepared for this question by having a broad, high-level knowledge of the company, its products, and its direction. To gain that knowledge, do your due diligence.

Almost all companies, whether publicly traded or privately owned, will have a website. Make sure you visit the company website to learn key facts about the company. Do not be the person who goes to the networking meeting or interview not having bothered to do any research. This demonstrates that you are not motivated or are just plain lazy, which is cause for immediate elimination.

Also, be sure to research any people you will meet while networking or in the interview. Look them up on LinkedIn, on the company website, and via other resources. If possible, seek out friends or acquaintances currently with or connected to the company who may be able to provide additional insights about the people you will meet. Be sure to write all of this information in your playbook as you gather it.

Practice Makes Perfect

If you want to be smooth, professional, and persuasive in your networking meetings and interviews, there's only one surefire approach to success: practice. Anticipate what you will be asked, develop succinct and appropriate responses, and practice them.

Time, Record, and Critique Your Answers

Now that you have an outline for your playbook, it's time to start filling in the necessary information. Once again, be careful not to make the serious mistake of talking too much.

Avoid this by writing down your responses to the questions you anticipate being asked and then timing your answers as you practice saying them out loud. *Timing your answers is critical.* The benefit of doing this is that you know the beginning of your story, the middle, and most importantly, the end. I had an incredibly extroverted coworker who didn't pick up on social cues, and had she been told to "thoroughly answer" a question, she'd have never stopped talking!

Generally speaking, when an interviewer asks you a question, your answer should be twenty to sixty seconds long. Most answers could even be as short as twenty to twenty-five seconds. If you talk longer, you are talking too much. Be aware that it is not just the answer you give but also the manner in which you answer that matters.

If you are being interviewed, it is because you have the credentials to do the job. For this reason, do not bombard your interviewer with long-winded stories about your accomplishments. Instead, do your best to identify the interviewer's problem and present your experience as the solution to that problem with short and relevant stories. It is tempting to tell everything you know about a subject, especially when you are talking about yourself, but over-talking can:

- Indicate to the interviewer that you are nervous

- Provide too much irrelevant and often damaging information

- Reveal scattered thinking and take you on unrelated tangents beyond what the interviewer wants to know

- Demonstrate that you do not have the ability to concisely state and support your case

- Waste valuable time, bore the interviewer, and reduce his interest in you as a viable candidate

- Exhibit a lack of respect for the interviewer by making the conversation all about you

Remember, it is *not* about you. It is about the interviewer and how you can solve his or her problems.

Once you have the timing down, rehearse the information in your playbook. Fine-tuning your answers to fit your personality and style will make them easier to remember in an actual networking or interview situation.

- Record and listen to your answers to determine whether they sound natural or stilted.

- Tweak your answers as needed, editing them until they sound the way you want them to.

- Continue to practice verbalizing your answers. Do not just go over them in your mind. They sound very different out loud compared with how they "sound" inside your head. Consider asking a friend or family member to listen to your answers and then critique you.

- Use a stopwatch and time yourself to ensure you are not talking too long. Remember, twenty to sixty seconds maximum per response.

- Answer the question exactly as you do in your playbook. Resist the temptation to ad lib. Keep your answers short, informative, and to the point. Include only critical information. Your interviewer's inquiries will tell you exactly what about your experience is important. Wait for that indicator before you respond with more information.

- Use a video camera to help you identify annoying gestures or filler phrases you may be using. Do you use your hands too much or not enough when you speak? Does "you know" creep into your verbiage? Do you fill space with non-words like "ummm" or audible pauses while you think of an answer? Watching yourself speak can be an eye-opening, or even downright terrifying, experience, but look at it as an opportunity to make improvements in your presentation.

- Imagine that you are performing at Carnegie Hall. You would not dream of showing up without practicing your material, would you?

The fact is, a networking meeting or an interview is like a performance at Carnegie Hall because it *is* a performance! You're memorizing lines, putting on a brave and friendly face, and attempting to win the approval of the crowd.

To do this effectively, you must practice, practice, practice. Listen to, refine, and repeat your answers until they become second nature. Listen to the recordings until you know your responses by heart. You can work with your playbook at home, in the car, at the airport, or even when working out at the gym.

I realize this type of preparation sounds extreme, but getting an interview is very hard work. Once you've obtained one, you cannot afford to blow it. In fact, you need to do all you can to nail it. Most of your competition is not going to put forth this type or amount of effort, which is why your success rate will be two to three times higher than your competition's.

An additional benefit to rehearsing and timing your answers is that you will become proficient in speaking in the twenty- to sixty-second sound bites I recommend. You will even develop an internal clock that will indicate to you when it's time to make your point and stop talking. Professional football quarterbacks develop mental timers that tell them when to get rid of the ball; a similar thing will happen to you. When you are asked a question you did not specifically prepare for, you will have both an internal clock running and memorized responses from your playbook from which to draw.

Case in point, I was recently invited to address the Texas Society of CPAs and to put together a two-hour seminar. To prepare, I wrote out my entire 14,000-word presentation and recorded it into my iPhone voice memo. For several months prior to the event, I listened to the presentation at home, in my car, on the way to appointments, and whenever I had downtime, such as waiting at the airport. As a result, I was able to fine-tune the content and deliver it with confidence in front of a large group of my peers while only occasionally referring to my notes. This greatly reduced my stress level and allowed me to remain confident and comfortable while speaking.

I cannot stress enough that you should never, ever go into a networking meeting or an interview unprepared. Instead, write out all the questions you think may be asked of you in your playbook, write out your answers to these questions, rehearse these answers out loud, and practice, practice, practice.

Know Your Own Background

"Know your own background" may seem painfully obvious. You might be thinking, "I don't need to prepare to discuss my background because I lived it!" However, you need to be able to recall your *best* experiences in a thorough and concise manner while networking or interviewing.

This is why it is so important to write out a short story for each position, experience, or bullet point on your résumé. Again, this twenty- to thirty-second short story will serve at least two purposes:

1. If the interviewer asks you about a specific experience, you will have a meaningful, thorough, concise story about that experience right at your fingertips.

2. You will have a broad database of your best experiences to draw on for any situation. In the event that you are asked a question for which you have not specifically prepared, this database will allow you to come up with a relevant short story.

All told, the playbook gives you a well-defined script that allows you to present yourself in the best possible light while answering critical job search questions. Start crafting yours today.

CHAPTER FOUR

Network for Success

Networking is one of the most reliable resources available to job seekers. Let me first explain what networking is by explaining what it is not.

Networking is not asking the person you are talking to for a job. Rather, networking is asking for advice and feedback in order to gain introductions to others who can aid you in your search for a job or who might be in a position to hire you for a job you are interested in and qualified for. A networking meeting might turn into an interview, as one meeting did for me, but that should not be your primary goal.

Networking can allow you to tap into the hidden job market and pinpoint those jobs that are not posted publicly but are revealed exclusively in the course of your pursuits. However, keep in mind that while the person with whom you are talking may be evaluating you prior to disclosing that they have an available position, you do not want to put them on the spot, as this can work to your disadvantage.

Your job search may afford you many networking opportunities, including one-on-one meetings or group functions. These meetings can be over the phone or in person. I believe that in person, one-on-one meetings are the most effective because the person gets a much better sense of who you are and what you bring to the table. If the other person is short on time but still wants to assist, they might suggest a phone meeting, which is a fine back up. When on the phone, be sure to be brief and concise in your answers, as people tend to have shorter attention spans on the phone.

Warm introductions are preferable to cold calls, but cold calls can still be productive, especially if you are able to establish a bridge or connection to that person. One cold call I made led to a seventeen-year career with two companies, which I will discuss in more detail at the end of this chapter.

Since most jobs come from personal referrals, networking means tapping into your business contacts, friends, and family for information. Other sources include your college alumni directory, professional association directories, veteran and military organizations, and church or civic groups. Do not limit yourself to a single group; work with several in order to gain exposure and a broad range of ideas about the job market.

Networking groups come in a lot of varieties, so finding one that matches your personality and your career goals is key. In some cases, your former company may include networking links as part of the exit package. However, more often than not, you are on your own. This is the time to reach out to others for leads, advice, and ideas.

Identify Your Goals

You should have four goals when networking:

1. To make connections with others who can help you

2. To gather information

3. To gain advice, feedback, and references

4. To generate insight and ideas

How do you make connections with others who can help you? Start by creating a list of names along with contact information, current titles, job descriptions, and resident companies or organizations. This is your "who's who" list of people who can possibly help you directly or offer introductions to those who might be able to assist you in your job search. These networking contacts will have fresh ideas for you to consider, ranging from how to better present yourself to which companies are hiring to what groups and individuals might provide the best networking opportunities for you.

Resist the temptation to assume who can and cannot help, and do not overlook those closest to you. I assumed my wife knew I wanted introductions to finance professionals, CFOs, and treasurers. Consequently, I did not make the most of her contacts or tell her how she could help me. After a meeting with an industry networking group, a job lead came my way that I was very interested in pursuing. I applied for the position and mentioned the opportunity to my wife, who promptly shocked me by saying, "That's interesting, because I know the treasurer!"

I thought I'd been thoroughly utilizing my network in order to increase my odds of a fruitful introduction, but I mistakenly did not consider my wife to be part of my network. When you are trying to either network your way into a company or simply gain an introduction, let everyone know and do not hesitate to ask for assistance, even from those closest to you!

This might sound obvious, but our brains are hardwired to make assumptions, and we do it thousands of times each day. It is a matter of safety to make an assumption on whether or not someone is going to stop at a red light or stay in his or her lane on the highway. We are constantly fed incomplete information, and our brains are designed to fill in the gaps.

The images below from the wonderful show *Brain Games* that airs on the National Geographic Channel are a good reminder of just how easy it is to make assumptions, and of how wrong we often are when we do so.

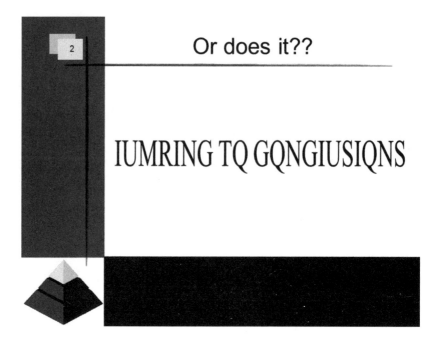

Or does it??

IUMRING TQ GQNGIUSIQNS

How did you do? If you're like most readers, you fell prey to the very human propensity to make assumptions. When you're searching for a job, this works against you, not for you. Make no assumptions when networking or interviewing, because you cannot possibly know every contact someone has or what job positions might be available. On numerous occasions, people I initially thought would be unable to help me wound up being invaluable resources. Obviously, some contacts and meetings will be productive and others will fall short of expectations. The key is to approach every meeting prepared for whatever may come.

A primary objective of each networking meeting is to see if the person with whom you are meeting has any contacts, either directly or indirectly, at your target list of companies or at others that may be similar to those on your list. A home run would be to walk out of each networking meeting with at least three additional introductions. After all, referrals are the lifeblood of networking.

In addition to company introductions, your contact might be able to offer a service (i.e., someone she knows enjoys reviewing résumés) or might be willing to mentor you. I met several people who assisted me in a variety of ways during my time in transition. This was due primarily to the fact that I was prepared, presented myself well, knew what I wanted, and respected their time. As a result, I was able to gain the tools I needed to quickly land my next opportunity.

Between 60–70% of your networking time should be spent with people who are employed. The remaining 30–40% should be spent with other people who are in transition, either in group settings or one-on-one meetings. This may sound counterintuitive. After all, what can you possibly gain from spending time with other people in transition?

The answer is contacts, information, and experience! Others in transition may be able to introduce you to contacts at your target company list. Also, you may be surprised by how much you can learn by observing how other people in transition approach the process and present themselves. You can then incorporate those lessons and best practices into your presentation of yourself. All told, making connections to others gives you access to information, advice, and feedback while generating essential insight and ideas.

More on Introductions

Before you reach out to your network or attend a networking meeting, dust off and polish the personal introduction first introduced in Chapter Two. This will allow you to come across as confident and organized. Again, this introduction is not the epic tale of your entire professional life, so pare it down to forty-five seconds. You do not want to lose your audience or waste their time.

In order to gain confidence and obtain productive feedback, practice this introduction with people you know. If you are part of a job search or training group, have someone ask you follow-up questions and be prepared with concise but thorough answers. When you have this down pat, ask your friends to throw tougher questions at you. These will keep you fresh and thinking about other possible questions you might be asked.

Also think about how you want others to introduce you to additional contacts and potential employers. This is something you can and should control. Write out a brief introduction of yourself that you can give or email to people to use when they are introducing you. Below is an example of an introduction I once sent to a networking contact to use when introducing me to a third person:

> *I would like to introduce you to Jay Fusaro. Jay has a very deep financial planning background and is a CPA. He has been very successful at leading and motivating teams on complex projects. He would greatly appreciate your advice and feedback regarding his search. Jay is seeking a position where he could lead the company's overall financial planning, forecasting, and performance management processes and provide analytical support to the CFO.*

Lead with Your Bio

As stated earlier, handing someone your résumé screams, "Find me a job!" For this reason, I strongly believe that the best tool to use when networking is the one-page bio. The bio is a much more user-friendly document that contains your competencies, attributes, résumé highlights, and most importantly, your target company list.

Build Rapport

Prior to meeting with your networking contact, study her on either LinkedIn, her company website, or Google in order to learn more about her. Research the company as well and be prepared to demonstrate that you took the time to learn about your contact and the company. This sign of respect demonstrates how serious you are about your job search. However, do not go overboard and rattle off all the information you attain in a single breath. Just be conversational and well informed.

One of the easiest ways to find common ground and build rapport is to reference the person who introduced you. This person is your first common link. For example, if your good friend Jack Youngblood introduced you to Mary Davis, your networking contact, you should open the conversation with "So Mary, how do you know Jack?" This is not only a nice reminder that your mutual friend Jack introduced the two of you but is also an effective icebreaker.

The next thing to look for are commonalities based on your contact's LinkedIn profile, company website, or other online resources. This could include where she grew up, attended school, or previously worked as well as what military ranks, board positions, hobbies, or sports interests she may have. For example, I grew up in New Jersey and went to school in Boston. When I look at someone's LinkedIn profile, I look for any connection they may have to the northeast that I can use in conversation.

Your alumni directory can also be an important tool in the networking aspect of your job search. View your alumni directory as an excellent resource from which to build your networking pipeline. When you begin an email or cold call a fellow alum, introduce yourself and mention that you attended the same school. Having established this bond, you can then ask if your contact would be willing to provide advice and feedback regarding your search. Most people are willing to take the time to meet and help fellow alumni. LinkedIn also has company alumni groups you can join.

Make the Most of Group Networking Meetings

Most people find group networking meetings unproductive, but it doesn't have to be this way. For starters, there are several ways to find the right group or groups for you. Ask your friends and colleagues what groups they enjoy attending, search LinkedIn for groups that are relevant to your industry, and of course ask your networking contacts what groups they believe would be beneficial to join. Don't overlook alumni groups, either! College, military, and even former employers frequently have alumni groups.

Make the most of such meetings by having a proper strategy going in. Often, in group settings, each attendee is given an opportunity to stand and speak. They recite their forty-five-second introduction, note the type of position they are looking for, and sit down. This approach usually does not result in any leads, and people typically leave feeling as though they have wasted their time.

Make these group meetings more productive by providing your introduction, discussing the type of work you are looking for, and asking if anyone has contacts at three or four of the companies on your target company list. Critical information just might surface. If you have a scheduled interview coming up, tell the group the name of the company you are interviewing with to see if anyone has a contact there and could be of assistance.

Be sure you have your bio, résumé, and business cards with you whenever you plan to attend any networking function, and also make sure you are connected on LinkedIn. This will allow you to make the most of the contacts you meet.

Group networking settings can also be a wonderful source of job search information. Not only are you on the lookout for potential connections and opportunities, but you can also seek better ways to present and package yourself. During networking meetings or any other related gatherings, always listen for information and phrases you can use in your own presentation.

Conversely, listen for things you should *not* say or do. Certain catchphrases, mannerisms, terminology, overblown talk, misused words, or even poor grammar can be enough to negatively influence a hiring authority.

For example, if you hear a great description, it is fair game to borrow and tailor it for your purposes, assuming you possess the skills and attributes being referenced. But if you hear this phrase too often in your networking circle, discard it. Like the latest pop tune, it may at first seem exciting and new but can quickly become predictable and tiresome.

Don't Bite Off More Than You Can Chew

You may believe you can conduct two to three networking meetings before lunch, but I argue that you will not be as prepared as you need to be for any of these networking meetings or for the required follow-up, including any "to-dos" and the required thank-you letters.

Recently, I met with a potential client who was very proud of the fact that he was conducting five networking meetings a day. I observed that while he was covering a great deal of territory, he was not getting as much traction as he could have been had he been better prepared for fewer meetings. He was spreading himself too thin but feeling a false sense of accomplishment simply because of the sheer volume of networking events he was completing.

If you are doing a thorough job of preparing beforehand by looking up each of your contacts on LinkedIn or other Internet sites as well as researching the company, adding the information to your playbook, and completing the requisite follow-up, you can only effectively manage two to three meetings per day. Keep in mind that you are no doubt simultaneously searching for opportunities on major career job boards and the job boards of your target companies.

All this takes time. Do not short-change yourself by skipping the research and preparation that are crucial to successful meetings, and under no circumstances should you forget to send follow-up thank-you notes. You simply must send a thank-you note to the person you met with and also to the person who made the introduction for you. This is a critical step for at least two reasons. First, you want to close the loop with the person who made the introduction. This individual wants to know if you ever met with the person he or she introduced you to, and it's rude not to be in touch in this regard. Second, you are always looking for a good reason to keep your name in front of people. A thank-you note is a great way to remind someone that you are still in the job market.

Be Mindful of Etiquette

Etiquette is always important, and networking meetings are no exception. For this reason, treat every networking meeting or interview like a guest/host relationship. You are the guest who is taking your cues from the host, your contact.

Mind Your Manners. Always begin and end each networking meeting or phone call with "Thank you for taking the time to meet (or speak) with me." In addition, it is imperative that you arrive on time. People are taking time out of their busy day to help you; show them respect by being on time. However, since unexpected things do happen and throw off the best of plans, be sure to have the person's contact information with you in the event that you are going to be late.

Ask if This is a Good Time to Talk. When calling someone, even if it's a scheduled call, always immediately ask if this is a good time to talk or if the call needs to be rescheduled for a more convenient time. Put your contact in control of helping you. After all, he might be answering the phone simply to tell you that he needs to reschedule.

If it's a cold call, do not rudely launch into your forty-five-second introduction the moment someone answers the phone. Say something like, "Hello, Mr. Smith, my name is Jay. Would you have a few minutes to talk with me? I would greatly appreciate your advice and feedback regarding my job search." Be respectful of other people's time and efforts to help.

Ask for Twenty Minutes. When you request a meeting with a networking contact, be respectful of that individual's time. I strongly suggest that you only ask for twenty minutes, whether you are meeting for coffee, over the phone, or in the office. Why just twenty minutes? Because everyone has twenty minutes available to help somebody.

Although you are only asking for twenty minutes, be prepared to use them well. Your thoughts should be concise and well organized, with no rambling and minimal ad libbing. When you are approaching the twenty-minute mark, check in with your host. Ask if you need to wrap up the meeting or if a few more minutes are permissible. The respect you show will be appreciated, and your host can inform you when the meeting needs to end. If your contact desires additional time to speak with you, an extension might be granted or an additional meeting can be suggested.

Choose Your Words Carefully. No one wants to be put on the spot, so be very sensitive about how you ask others for help when approaching them in a networking situation. I strongly recommend that my clients ask for "advice and feedback" and that they avoid the distasteful phrase "pick your brain," which is overused and conjures up an unpleasant image. Likewise, they should never ask networking contacts at the outset if they "know of any job openings."

Obviously, if contacts believe you are a good candidate, they will share their leads. You simply do not want to make them uncomfortable or put them in the position of having to say "No" to you. Your networking contacts want to help you. Make it easy by asking for advice and feedback and do not put them on the spot.

For example, which of the following telephone calls would you find more effective?

Hi Jay. I was referred to you by Bob Smith. I would really appreciate your advice and feedback regarding my search. Do you have twenty or so minutes this week to get together?

or

Can we get together? I'd like to pick your brain. Also, do you know of any job openings?

I believe the choice is clear. Besides, who doesn't like being asked for their advice and feedback? The person you're asking will not feel threatened or pressured. In fact, he will most likely believe that he can deliver the advice you need and will look forward to helping you.

Summarize the "To-Do" List. Before you conclude a networking meeting, summarize any next steps you discussed and make sure you have a clear understanding of any follow-up items that need the attention of you or your contact. This individual is likely very busy and may forget what he offered to do, so politely remind him that you are looking forward to the introductions he offered to make on your behalf.

Exchange Business Cards. If the networking meeting or interview is conducted in person, be sure to conclude the meeting by asking for a business card from each person with whom you meet so that you can send a follow-up thank-you note. Remember to bring plenty of your own business cards as well to give in return.

Send a Thank-You Note. Always send a thank-you note or email to the person with whom you met. If you need a refresher on how to write a proper thank-you note, refer back to Chapter Two.

In this thank-you note, as appropriate, offer a polite reminder that you are looking forward to receiving the introductions your host offered to make.

Likewise, as mentioned, it's imperative to send a thank-you note to the person who introduced you to your networking or interview contact.

One caveat: do not use blast or group emails to remind people that you are still in transition, as these are neither professional nor effective.

Dress Appropriately. It might be nice to think that we are not judged on outward appearances, but the truth of course is that we are. You would never send out a résumé on crumpled, coffee-stained paper. In the same vein, how you dress is another indicator of how you will be perceived. As has often been said, "You only get one chance to make a good first impression."

More to the point, in a networking meeting, you are asking your contact to make introductions on your behalf. For this reason, it is critical to look as professional for this meeting as you do for an interview. Your contact may be reluctant to offer referrals if you show up in attire that is too casual because it sends the message that you are not taking your job search seriously. If *you* are not serious about your job search, why should your contact be?

Recently, an experienced professional and I met for a networking meeting. I dressed in professional attire and expected him to do the same. I was very surprised when he showed up in a t-shirt and baseball cap. As a result, I was reluctant to provide any introductions for him because of my concern that he might show up in similar attire when meeting my contacts. That clearly would be unacceptable as well as disrespectful and would reflect poorly on me.

The fact is, you are judged in several ways beginning the moment you walk into a networking meeting or interview. Do you exude confidence? Do you look the part of a person who can represent the company in the best possible way? Do you fit the role the company has in mind?

Make your first impression the best one possible by dressing in a professional manner regardless of whether you are networking or interviewing. Men should wear a jacket and tie, and women should wear corresponding business attire. You never know who you might meet, so show respect and be prepared.

I admit that I am a stereotypical guy with very little fashion sense. My former company had a "business casual" policy, so when I found myself in transition, my wardrobe lacked formal business attire. One of the smartest moves I made was meeting with a fashion consultant about my clothing options. One of the first things Julie Bartlett of Colour IQ told me is that when you wear a suit or a jacket and tie, it shows that you are serious. Business casual is just that, a "casual" approach to your search. Your search is not and should not be a casual endeavor. While most of the wardrobe pieces that follow have budget-friendly options, those that require spending a bit more money will be well worth the investment.

For Men. Unless you are told specifically to dress down, it is best to wear a suit. Even if the job is in a business casual environment, dressing the part of upper management shows respect for the company and the position you are hoping to win. Choose a suit in a dark color like black, charcoal, gray, or navy. Finish the look with a belt in a similar color. Make sure your belt looks fresh and does not show crease marks due to either weight gain or loss. You never know when the hiring authority will be at a networking group meeting, so be ready. Nice slacks and a sport coat may seem like a good option, but they still reflect a more casual attitude.

The shirt you choose is equally important. Choose a solid white, pale blue, or even light gray with long sleeves. The color choice should coordinate with the suit you are wearing. Do *not* wear a button-down collar. This will make the finest suit instantly look more casual. In addition, be sure the shirt fits properly. I have interviewed candidates for top corporate positions who left the top buttons of their shirt collars undone because their shirts were too small. This is very unprofessional.

A patterned tie with a small print or stripe maintains a professional look, but keep the colors sedate to coordinate with the suit. Colors like gray, maroon, navy, burgundy, medium blue, and even a light pastel can lend a professional look without being too stuffy or formal.

A simple choice of shoe type can also make or break a look. Always choose shoes that tie over loafers. As my fashion consultant said, "Loafers are for loafing. That's not the image you want to convey." Be sure your shoes are shining and have been recently polished for each interview, and coordinate sock color with shoe color. Black is always a safe option.

As far as jewelry is concerned, the best option is a simple watch and at most a ring or two.

Good grooming is an essential part of dressing for the interview. Make sure your hair (including facial hair) is professionally trimmed. Fingernails should likewise be neatly trimmed and clean. It may sound frivolous, but a professional manicure can make a big difference, since messy cuticles or grubby nails create a negative image.

Use aftershave or cologne in moderation or avoid them altogether. If the person interviewing you is sensitive to fragrances and yours is too strong, it can cost you the job. It is better to leave the scent off than risk overdoing it.

Finish your look with a professional-looking briefcase or portfolio, and make sure you bring additional copies of your bio, résumé, business cards, a list of references, and other important materials you might need.

For Women. Women have a bit more flexibility in choosing the look they want to convey, but unless interviewing with a company in the fashion industry, it is safer to maintain a conservative, professional appearance. The initial meeting should be about networking or the interview, not about wardrobes or figures.

Suits are fine. Skirts should be long enough to sit comfortably. This means somewhere near the knee, slightly above or below. No mini- or mid-thigh skirts, and certainly no tight-fitting skirts that hug every curve. Simple, clean lines without too many fussy details are best. Slacks should be tailored, not tight or loose and flowing. A dress with a matching jacket works well, too.

If you decide on a suit, choose a coordinating blouse. White is always a good option, but many solid colors work well. Whatever your choice, opt for more conservative colors, and make sure the cut of the blouse is not revealing. Many companies have specific rules about cleavage. Tight or low-cut blouses do not fit into corporate environments, especially those with a more conservative client base.

Choose closed-toe shoes over sandals, keep the heel height to a maximum of three inches, and coordinate the shoe color with the outfit.

Limit jewelry, and avoid anything that rattles, jangles, or makes noise when you move. This means no charm bracelets, stacks of bangles, or oversized necklaces and earrings. These can be very distracting.

As needed, consider updating your hairstyle for a more professional look, and be aware that conservative companies may have strict guidelines about hair color. Even if you are interviewing in a highly creative field, wait until you know how the company feels about neon red tresses or purple stripes before you decide this is a good option.

Good grooming is also essential. Keep makeup to a minimum and avoid outlandish colors. Find a friend who can help you polish your look or make an appointment with a department store makeup counter. Go easy on the perfume. Manicured nails, whether professionally done or part of your regular routine, are essential, but save the bright neon colors for another time and place.

Choose a smaller purse or even one that will fit inside a professional-looking briefcase. Trying to juggle a briefcase or portfolio plus a huge purse can be a challenge. Bring copies of your bio, résumé, business cards, a list of references, and other important materials you might need.

Know How Your Contacts Can Help You

One question people are asked over and over when networking is, "How can I help you?" This may sound like a simple question, but many people do not know how to answer it. At first, I too had a difficult time answering this question effectively.

Common poor answers include the following:

- "Do you know of any job openings?"

- "Do you know anyone who can use someone with my skill set?"

- "Could you introduce me to your boss?"

Invariably, these responses put the other person in an awkward position and the initial response is usually, "*No, I do* [or can] *not.*"

When someone asks how they can help you, you need to be able to answer the question appropriately! One of the best ways to do this is to provide your target company list and ask if your contact knows of anyone who works at these companies or in similar industries, but make it clear that this list is a work in progress. For example, if JCPenney is on your list and your contact says, "I don't know anyone at JCPenney, but I do know someone at Neiman Marcus; would that work?" — your response would be, "Of course; that's perfect!"

A target list of specific companies is better than a general reference to various industries because it's easier for someone to recall a specific contact at a specific company than it is for them to scour their brain for an industry acquaintance. For example, I was recently asked if I knew anyone in the high-tech industry. No one came to mind. However, when asked if I knew someone at IBM, I immediately thought of a good friend who works there. The specific reminder helped jog my memory.

If you have adequately prepared for your networking meeting and have behaved and dressed appropriately, it is likely that the person with whom you are networking will be happy to make introductions on your behalf, provided they know someone at one of your target companies or a similar company.

An additional question you need to be prepared for is "What are you looking for?" As with "Tell me about yourself," your answer should be no more than forty-five seconds long. Simply reply with the type of position you are seeking and two or three skills you want to emphasize. As discussed, if you are struggling for the right words in your response, seek out key terms and phrases from applicable job descriptions and include them in your description.

Networking is a Two-Way Street

During my initial time in transition, I did not think I had anything to offer the person I was networking with until one of my mentors told me I should always be prepared to ask the "How can I help you?" question, too.

You may not believe you have something to offer when you are in transition, but you do. You have contacts, introductions, and information. By taking the time to ask how you can help the person who is helping you, you demonstrate that you are not only thinking of yourself. Believe me, you do not want to be thought of as a "taker" but as someone who gives back as well.

Most people in transition become very self-absorbed (me included!). Be mindful of this and work to balance it. Near the end of your networking meeting, say, "Thank you for taking the time to meet with me. I really appreciate it. Is there anything I can do to help you?"

Whether or not you can actually help the other person is irrelevant. The point is that you have offered to help. The person you are working with will remember that gesture, and it will leave a lasting positive impression.

Prior to asking this question for the first time in a networking meeting, I did not expect anything to come of it. I was having lunch with a very successful partner in a private equity firm, and I remember thinking to myself, "What do I have to offer this person? Here I am in transition, and he is a successfully employed business executive."

As our lunch was nearing a close, I thought, "Why not ask anyway?" Out loud, I said, "Peter, thank you for taking the time to meet with me; I really appreciate it. Tell me, is there anything I can do to help you?"

To my surprise, he said, "As a matter of fact, one of my clients would like an introduction to an executive with your former employer. Could you facilitate that?"

My contact was willing to help me, and it was only right that I offered to help him. I made the introduction, and his client wound up doing a business deal with the company. This type of situation might be atypical, but it can happen. Besides, asking if you can help is just the right thing to do.

Job Lead Sharing

Sometimes, networking includes sharing job leads with others. This may sound counterintuitive, considering that you are in competition with many others for the same positions, but other candidates may have a unique set of skills that will fit a position better than your skill set. Conversely, these other candidates may be interviewing for a position that is perfect for you.

Back in the days before the Internet, job seekers searched the Sunday classifieds for the latest jobs. All they had to do was spend a few hours going through each listing to find the one that fit them and their qualifications best. Hardly anyone shared leads, and the race was on to see who could apply first.

Today, all that has changed. If it's on the Internet, it's fair game for all job seekers. Thousands of jobs are posted, and each may pull in hundreds or even thousands of résumés. Most candidates do not come anywhere near meeting all the requirements, but that doesn't stop the influx of résumés that can be sent with the click of a mouse. Needless to say, HR professionals and hiring authorities have grown pretty skeptical about a good portion of the résumés that show up in their inboxes.

In my opinion, job lead sharing provides benefits that far outweigh any potential loss of opportunity. When I was in transition, I met and joined forces with several others in transition. We shared leads, we coached each other before interviews, and we found that we covered much more territory by sourcing and researching leads together than by going it alone. I firmly believe that job lead sharing does *not* reduce your chances of getting an interview or an offer. Either the position is a fit for you or it is not.

Case in point, I met a very good friend through a networking group. Since we both had accounting backgrounds, we decided to give job lead sharing a try. Occasionally, we found a job that both of us applied for, and we took the process to the next level by actually coaching each other for the interview for the same position.

At one point, we both made it to the first round of interviews with the same company. I was scheduled to go first, so when my interview was over, I gave my friend insight on how to approach his interview. When we both made it to the second round, he went first and coached me on the questions they asked him. By the third round, we were both still among the final candidates. Before the final interviews took place, I received an offer from a different company I had been pursuing, so I withdrew my candidacy but continued to help him. He went on the interview, performed well, and was offered the position. While our backgrounds were similar, he was actually a better match for the employer's requirements. However, I believe our working together helped both of us to be better prepared.

In order for job sharing to work well, be mindful of the following essential elements:

- Your partner(s) should be a person you trust.

- Leads should go both ways, which means a non-contributing partner(s) should be removed.

An additional benefit of sharing job leads is that when you help someone, you feel better about yourself.

No Pressure (but Be Prepared for Anything)

Since networking meetings are not formal interviews, they should be more relaxed than interviews. After all, you are asking for "advice and feedback." However, as the story below makes clear, there's always the chance that a meeting can turn into an interview if your networking contact decides to consider you for an open position. The moral of the story is to be prepared for anything. Use these meetings as opportunities to practice your interview skills (developed in Part II), and make sure your professional appearance is always up to snuff.

Early in my career, I cold-called the CFO of Comerica Bank Texas looking for his advice and feedback regarding my search. He agreed to meet with me at a later date for twenty minutes. Due to his high position in the bank, I approached the meeting as though it were an interview both in my preparation and in how I dressed, which meant I did extensive research on Comerica and wore a business suit and tie.

The CFO greeted me as I got off the elevator on his floor. After exchanging pleasantries, I asked how the integration of a recent acquisition was proceeding. Our conversation about the bank continued from the elevator to the conference room. By the time we sat down, he knew I was very serious about both our meeting and my job search.

Once we had established chemistry and my technical competence, the CFO mentioned that someone with a background similar to mine had resigned from the bank two weeks prior. He then asked if I had time during our meeting to visit with some other people who reported directly to him.

What started as a simple twenty-minute "advice and feedback" meeting turned into a full-blown interview. I came prepared with information about the bank and my short stories on how my experience would allow me to make a significant contribution to the work environment. As a result of my preparation, I moved forward in the interview process and was offered a position with the bank.

In hindsight, I had zero competition for a position unknown to me at the time of my networking meeting. In other words, a job I didn't know existed was mine to lose. It's safe to assume the CFO would not have shared the opening had I arrived unprepared, had I failed to establish rapport, or had I not been technically competent.

Such opportunities do exist, and it only takes one meeting like this to make all the difference in the world. That is the challenge of networking — not the meeting itself, but the comprehensive preparation and the hope that the meeting is fruitful.

By the way, when that Comerica CFO advanced to another company, he asked me to join him there. Being fully prepared at our initial meeting thus resulted in a seventeen-year run with two companies.

Prepare for each networking meeting as if there were a job available. You never know; there just might be.

PART II

Interviewing

Congratulations! You've been contacted for an interview. Your initial hard work has paid off, and now it's show time. Interview lengths vary, but it's common to only have an audience with the interviewer for an hour or less. You need to make every minute count, and this section shows you how to do that.

The interview is your chance to show the potential employer that you are the best person for the position. Keep in mind that you would not be on the interview if the employer did not believe that on paper (i.e., your résumé) you could do the job. Now is the time to demonstrate your technical competence and your ability to build chemistry with others.

CHAPTER FIVE

Separate Yourself from the Competition

I t's impossible to exaggerate the importance of the interview and the necessity of separating yourself from the competition. In addition to the material presented in Part I of this book, you can significantly improve your chances of interviewing well by preparing in advance for the different types of interviewers and interviewing styles you may encounter. The fact is, if you wish to achieve optimal success, each must be approached in a slightly different manner.

Four Types of Interviewers

The four major decision makers you may run across in your interview process are as follows:

- Human resources (HR) managers or professionals

- Hiring managers

- Potential future peers

- Internal customers

Candidates often make the mistake of preparing for these four types of interviewers as if they were the same, but this is seldom effective because, the truth is, each of these four types will approach the interview from a different perspective.

Human Resources

In many companies, the trained HR professional is not gauging your technical competence to perform the job. Rather, this individual is judging your attitude to see if you are a good fit for the company culture. The HR professional will do this by asking questions of a situational or behavioral orientation or questions designed to assess your attitude.

Be sure to respond appropriately when asked a situational question. This is a time, either real or hypothetical, when you have been placed in an uncomfortable or stressful situation. Examples of situational questions and prompts include the following:

- Tell me about a time you worked for a difficult boss (or a tough professor, if you are a recent graduate).

- What is the most difficult problem you have faced, and what was the solution to that problem?

- Tell me about a time you had to work in a difficult environment. What was the outcome?

Oftentimes, the interviewer is attempting to gauge your attitude toward the situation more than your actual answer. Thus, you want your responses to be constructed in a thoughtful, compassionate, rational way. Keep in mind that the interview process is not a confessional. Stay away from answers such as, *"Now that you ask, I did work for this one boss ... He was horrible and nobody liked him; it wasn't just me."* An answer like this could immediately eliminate you from consideration.

Likewise, if you have ever had to fire someone, do not go into the painful, gory details. Instead, stress how you followed corporate policy and procedures and how, in the long term, the move benefited the team and the company.

Questions designed to assess your attitude usually follow this line of questioning:

- Did you ever have disagreements with your boss, professor, co-workers, or team members?

- What are some assumptions that have been made about you that you think are incorrect?

- Why did you leave your previous company (or any of the companies on your résumé)?

Effective answers include the following:

- "We do not have disagreements; we have discussions and healthy debates. Sometimes the decision goes my preferred way, sometimes not, and often it's a blend."

- "People believe that because I'm a nice person, I'm also a doormat, and that is not the case."

I address the important topic of appropriately answering why you left your previous company at length later in this chapter, but suffice it to say, it pays to craft a careful answer to this question.

Because it is the job of human resources to determine whether or not you will fit into the company culture, be aware that these professionals may want to catch you off guard once the interview seems to be over. For example, to get you out of your comfort zone once the "formal" interview concludes, you may be asked to take what appears to be an office tour. This is when you are most likely to lower your guard and make a mistake. Do not let this happen; never turn off your interview mode until you have left the premises.

Hiring Manager

The hiring authority will most likely have an entirely different approach to the interview and may not be as skilled an interviewer as someone from human resources. As a result, you must approach these two individuals very differently. The hiring manager will be looking for direct examples of how you can solve the company's problems. Again, understanding this is key to a successful interview.

Keep in mind that it is common for a hiring manager to ask you about a competency or a skill that you do not possess. If this happens, as it did to me, do not lie or misrepresent yourself. Take the question head-on and offer something to the effect of, "I do not have that particular skill, but I feel confident that I could either learn it or hire/consult subject matter experts in that area."

The hiring manager may already know from your résumé that you do not possess this particular knowledge or skill set. In fact, she may want to see how easily you become flummoxed or rattled or, worse, if you will lie about your skills and experience.

Potential Peers

Peers basically want to know if you play well with others. In other words, what kind of teammate are you going to be? Are you someone your potential future colleagues are going to want to work with eight to ten hours a day?

To be successful in peer interviews, prepare examples about working in a team environment and being supportive of others.

Internal Customers

Internal customers are those whom you or your team will provide internal support services to. Internal customers are not going to be as concerned about your technical competence to do the job. Instead, such interviewers are more interested in your:

- Attitude toward providing customer service

- Responsiveness

- Ability to listen

- Desire to understand their business

- "Fit" as a business partner

Consequently, your examples will need to address those primary concerns. The key to success is knowing that you need to approach each person you meet during the interview process differently. Always be keenly aware that this process is about them, not you!

Different Interview Styles

In addition to different types of interviewers, you also need to be prepared for different interview styles based on personality. The four general personality types you might encounter include the following:

- Leaders

- Analyticals

- Creatives

- Altruistics

Your particular personality type may mesh perfectly with some of the people you will be interviewing or networking with. Alternatively, your personality could be off-putting to others. While this does not mean there is something wrong with you, it does mean that you might not connect as readily or as easily or that you won't create the type of chemistry that will result in a job offer. Understanding this up front can help you mindfully avoid problems.

Leaders

Leaders are the "take charge" individuals you would follow into battle, corporate or otherwise, and they tend to use strong, forceful language. Depending on the position you are applying for, you may or may not encounter them in the initial interview; but as you progress, your likelihood of encountering leaders increases. You should never attempt to lock horns with these individuals for any reason. Instead, your goal should be to develop a dialogue and gain knowledge regarding the corporate strategy and structure, both of which are important to leaders.

Analyticals

These are detail-oriented people; they want all the facts when making decisions, and they are not limited to individuals in the accounting, finance, or legal departments. When answering their questions, make sure you have your facts straight and that you provide well-thought-out answers. Your playbook preparation will be a crucial asset during the interview process with such personalities. Be sure you can convey what you have done in the past that involved clear thinking and research to make an intelligent decision.

Creatives

The creative department may involve everyone from marketing to the writers and designers who are hands-on with the products and services the company provides. Likely to be the "fun crowd," they will be interested in how you think outside the box (or even kick it to the curb).

Altruistics

These team members want to make everything better in and for the big picture, and teamwork is central to their business philosophy. Their questions will often center on what you bring to the table to benefit the team. People who fall into this category are often very concerned about the welfare of others. If you believe this is the perspective of the person you are talking to, be prepared with appropriate stories. Give examples of how you have helped coworkers be more successful or worked overtime without being asked to assist either a manager or a direct report. If you are involved with any nonprofit organizations, this would be a good time to bring it up in conversation.

Like you, interviewers are made up of different personality types or even varying degrees of each personality type. Think of different ways you can answer the same question for each type of interviewer, and you will be better prepared to move quickly and successfully from one type to another.

Initial Prep Work

When you are contacted to schedule an interview, be sure to ask about the expected agenda and duration of the meeting as well as the names and positions of the people with whom you are going to meet. Sometimes companies won't share this information with you, but knowing whether the interview will last thirty minutes or three hours can make a huge difference in your preparation.

If you haven't already done so, thoroughly research the company. This will provide you with a wealth of information. Often, an interviewer will open with "What do you know about our company?" You need to be prepared for this question by having a broad, high-level knowledge of the company, its products, and its direction.

This information will also help you formulate questions you can ask and allow you to demonstrate that you have done your homework. Prepare at least three talking points based on the information you have gathered. Typically, a candidate will only have the time to raise one to three key points, but asking smart questions can set you apart from the competition.

If you are able to get their names, research the people you will meet for the interview. Look them up on LinkedIn, the company website, and other resources. If possible, seek out friends or acquaintances currently with the company who may be able to provide additional insights about the people you will be talking to.

In anticipation of the rapport you will try to build with the interviewer, look for common denominators you can use as icebreakers. This can include where they went to school, previous places of employment, or hobbies and interests. Making a connection and establishing a bond can help build chemistry between you and the interviewer. This can be an important factor in your advancement toward the next step of the interview process.

By taking the time to do your due diligence, you demonstrate a good work ethic, strong interest in the company, and respect for the interviewer. This goes a long way toward building rapport and making a good impression.

Use That Playbook

Now that you have developed your playbook, it's time to put it to use. After all, this is the foundation you have been building to help you successfully answer questions and more effectively present yourself in an interview. Make sure your playbook contains the following:

1. Your answers to "Tell me about yourself" and "Take me through your résumé"

2. Your answer to "What are you looking for?"

3. Your top three strengths and one weakness

4. Your top three key accomplishments

5. Your answers to situational questions

6. Your answers to behavioral questions

7. Your top three key success stories using the "SAR" approach (**S**ituation, **A**ction, **R**esult) and the impact you had on the outcome (think of these as brief career competency stories)

8. Your company research or due diligence

9. Your top three reasons why you are interested in a particular company

10. Why you left a company or why you want to leave your current company (to be discussed in this section)

11. The compensation you seek (to be discussed in this section)

12. Short stories (twenty to thirty seconds each) for every bullet point on your résumé

Master the Power of Three

Lee Colan and Julie Davis-Colan in their bestselling book *Stick with It: Mastering the Art of Adherence* explain that most people think in threes. This is why, after you read a specific company's description of the position you are applying for, you should choose three bullet points from your résumé that align with the qualities or requirements listed in that description and prepare to discuss them. For example, when asked about your strengths, you might explain that you are solutions focused and that you excel in team leadership and creative problem solving. Three items offer a complete list, and this simply feels right. A greater number gives too much information, and fewer than three sounds incomplete.

Likewise, when asked to talk about your accomplishments, list your top three in a brief, bullet-point type of format. Typically, the interviewer will pick which one(s) he or she wants to learn more about, thus allowing you to present the appropriate short story.

Do not answer the question with your accomplishment and your story, another accomplishment and story, then another accomplishment and story. You do not want to come across as long-winded or self-absorbed. Remember, this is not about you. You are there to solve the interviewer's problem, not to talk about how great you are or to provide irrelevant information.

Remember that your playbook will constantly be evolving. For example, if you are stumped by a question or hear a great answer you hadn't previously thought of while on an interview or in a networking meeting, that information should go in your playbook. Remember to always record and play back your answers until they become second nature.

Also remember that the reason you are following a playbook is that people tend to talk too much in interviews, offering extraneous, irrelevant, and often damaging information. As discussed earlier, detrimental information can eliminate you from consideration.

It is often said that competence gets you the interview while likeability gets you hired. It is easier to be likeable when you are not nervous but instead are properly prepared. Know and follow your playbook, and you are more likely to be confident, relaxed, and successful.

Body Language

As mentioned previously, the interview process is similar to the relationship between a guest and host. The interviewer is the host, and your job is to be a good guest. To make a good impression, follow these guidelines:

- **Make good eye contact and use a strong handshake.** But be careful — do not crush the interviewer's hand. By the same token, do not give a limp handshake. Use your whole hand, not just your fingertips.

- **Smile.** Smile with your eyes as well as your mouth, and be genuine with your smile. This will also help you to relax.

- **Be mindful of your posture.** This means shoulders back, head up, chest out, and no slouching. Slouching conveys disinterest and is rude.

- **Convey a positive attitude.** People cannot help but be attracted to positive individuals. The interviewer does not need to know if you are having a bad day.

- **Be high energy.** You do not have to be a cheerleader, just be genuinely enthusiastic.

- **Subtly "mirror" the mannerisms of the interviewer.** If he leans forward, you lean forward. If she crosses her legs, you cross your legs. If he lowers his voice, you do the same. Be subtle, but do attempt to mirror the interviewer's body language.

In sum, the image you want to project to the interviewer is:

- I am a professional.

- I have no problems.

- I create no problems.

- I will solve all your problems.

- I am focused, competent, and passionate.

If you can do this, you are well on your way to a job offer.

Addressing the Big Four Questions

Assuming you are technically competent and that chemistry exists between you and the interviewer, a successful interview often depends on how you address what I call the "big four."

After interviewing several hundred hiring managers, my mentor Jim Ashworth discovered that candidates typically fail to move forward in the process and receive an offer because they do not adequately address one or more of the following four issues:

1. Effectively answering, "Tell me about yourself" as developed in Chapter One

2. Demonstrating a high level of enthusiasm

3. Providing a sensible, succinct answer as to why they left their last position
    (or any position on their résumé)

4. Effectively discussing desired compensation

If you are technically competent to do the job, have developed chemistry with the interviewer, and effectively address all four of these topics, your likelihood of moving forward in the interview process increases significantly. Alternatively, your inability to effectively handle any of these four issues can destroy your chances, so let's discuss the ins and outs of each of these issues.

Answering "Tell Me about Yourself"

As mentioned in Chapter One, your response to this prompt is often called your elevator speech. The interviewer is most likely asking this question to kick off the interview. Alternatively, she may ask you to take her through your résumé. These are the two most common methods interviewers use to start a discussion.

Again, the interviewer is not asking this question to learn the details of your life or to hear how great you are. She is actually asking the question to determine whether you can speak concisely. If she wants more detailed information regarding anything on your résumé, she will ask for it.

Your response to this question should be slightly different in an interview than it would be during a networking meeting. In an interview, your answer should be tailored to the specific opportunity you are seeking. In any event, your answer should be approximately forty-five seconds long. Make it impactful, high-level, concise, and relevant.

As explained in Chapter One, divide your introduction into three segments. The first segment should be about the past:

> *I grew up in New Jersey through high school and attended college in Boston at Northeastern University. I relocated to Dallas in 1991.*

Saying this takes under ten seconds and is all the interviewer really wants to know.

The next segment covers your last position and should include two or three relevant examples from a recent position that are directly relatable to the position for which you are applying:

> *I have my CPA, and most recently I have been very successful at leading and motivating teams*

on complex projects. I have both IPO and M&A experience, and I was head of Corporate Planning for a publicly traded $3B company.

The last segment should detail what you are looking for in your next opportunity and can include two or three things from the job description that genuinely excite you about the opportunity you are interviewing for:

I am seeking a position where I can lead the company's overall financial planning, forecasting, and performance management process and also provide the CFO with visibility and predictability in earnings in order to elevate the quality of information presented to both senior management and Wall Street.

Common fatal missteps in answering this question are bloviating, stammering, or generally lacking preparation. This is not the time to tell the interviewer all the details of your personal and professional life. In fact, this is a surefire way to be eliminated from the competition.

Demonstrating Enthusiasm

Demonstrating a high level of enthusiasm is the second of the "big four" job interview issues. One way to effectively generate authentic enthusiasm about a position is to get a copy of the job description prior to the interview and pick out two things that genuinely excite you. Then, tie those two things into your background to craft what I call your enthusiasm statement.

If you have the opportunity, deliver this enthusiasm statement early in the interview process. Before the interview even begins, perhaps when you are walking to the conference room with your interviewer, you might consider saying something like:

> *Ms. Smith, I just want you to know before we get started that I am very interested in this position. After reviewing the job description, particularly the bit about working with the CFO and providing earnings guidance, I believe that I have the knowledge, skills, and ability to make a significant contribution to your team.*

Alternatively, if you do not have a job description but have talked with a recruiter, you might consider saying something like this:

After talking with the recruiter, I am very excited about this opportunity, and I believe I have the knowledge, skills, and ability to make a significant impact on your team.

Be prepared for the other person to be slightly uncomfortable after you deliver this statement, most likely because it is not a common component of most interviews. But remember, your job is to put that person at ease. After you deliver your enthusiasm statement, this individual might say, "I'm glad you really want the job, but we still need to go through the interview process." To that, simply say, "I understand; I just wanted you to know that I am very interested in the position." Deliver this statement to each person you interview with.

Often, as a hiring manager, I wasn't certain whether candidates truly wanted the job because they didn't demonstrate enough enthusiasm. As you can surmise, such candidates were less likely to advance. If you are not interested in the job, why are you on the interview? State your enthusiasm for the position and tie it to your ability to make a significant contribution.

Conveying Why You Left Your Last Position

This is the third of the four critical interview issues, and it will likely be asked in one of the following ways:

- Why did you leave your last position?

- Why do you want to leave your current position?

- Why did you leave any position on your résumé?

You need to have a scripted answer for each of these scenarios in your playbook. If you do not effectively answer this question, you may be eliminated from contention. Usually, someone from HR asks why you left or want to leave a given position. As discussed, HR is looking to assess your "attitude and fit" for the company culture and position. HR may not necessarily be qualified to judge your technical competence, but it usually has a very big say in your fit. Thus, it is important to understand that the "why you left" question is an *attitude* question. To answer it, incorporate the following tips:

- Your response should be no longer than for-ty-five seconds in length. Write it out in your playbook and memorize it. It should be short and sweet, with no babbling or ad libbing, and it should provide little detail. Remember, the interview is not a confessional.

- Emphasize that you left this position (or want to leave your current position) due to no fault of the company or your boss. Do not come across as someone who is a victim or who assigns blame to others. My friend Lee Colan passed along an acronym that I believe is appropriate in this situation: **T.H.I.N.K.** In other words, your answer to this question needs to be **T**rue, **H**elpful, **I**nspiring, **N**ecessary, and most of all **K**ind, to others as well as to yourself.

To convey a positive attitude when asked why you left a former position, speak in a warm and friend-ly tone with something like, "I'm glad you asked." In-stantly, your answer turns what is often an uncomfort-able question into the start of a positive story. Now the interviewer cannot wait to hear what you have to say.

Continue with something positive about your last or current position and state the reason you are seeking new employment. My response went something like this:

> *I had the privilege of working with Alliance Data for the best twelve years of my career. As a matter of fact, both my former boss and the current CEO are two of my mentors. I thoroughly enjoyed my time with Alliance and am proud of my accomplishments there. A new CFO was hired, and he decided to change the direction of the department and bring in his own team. As a result, along with several others in the senior finance team, I left the company. I had a great experience.*

A solid answer to "Why do you want to leave your current position?" is as follows:

> *I really enjoy my current position, but when I heard about this opportunity, it really excited me. Specifically, I am interested in … [name three things about the new job that excite you]. I believe I have the knowledge and skills to make a significant contribution to your team.*

Remember, you are a positive person, a team player, and you get along with your boss and your peers. Even if you are bitter, this is not the time or place to express that sentiment. If you have a poor attitude toward a former employer, boss, or professor, chances are you will bring that same bad attitude to your next employer. If the interviewer detects even a whiff of a bad attitude, you will be eliminated from contention.

I know, because I have eliminated multiple candidates for this very reason. Also, sadly, I know of several very competent people who did not advance in the interview process because of this, even though they were extremely well qualified for the positions they were applying for.

Discussing Compensation

Many books have been written about the topic of compensation. It is an important one, and you need to be comfortable with your approach.

Compensation questions are most often asked in one of two ways: "What are you looking to make in your next opportunity?" or "How much are you currently making?"

As I have consistently advocated throughout this book, scripting out your answers is critical to your success during interviews, and this aspect of the interview is no exception. Compensation is typically brought up when you are talking to the person in Human Resources. In rare circumstances, compensation is not raised until an offer is extended. Regardless, the candidate should never raise the compensation issue first; the employer should always introduce the topic. Your job is to be prepared whenever it comes up.

If you are asked, "What are you looking to make in your next opportunity?" I strongly recommend that you answer the question directly. Never answer with, "I trust that you will pay me fairly" or "We can discuss this later." The interviewer wants to know your answer, and you should know if the job for which you are applying will meet your earnings expectations.

I also suggest you offer a monetary range rather than a specific dollar amount. Ideally, you should know or have some idea as to the standard compensation range of the position. If you do not, do some research to determine the market salary range of the position.

Examples of compensation ranges are as follows:

- If you believe the position pays $8/hour, suggest $8 to $9/hour.

- If you believe the position pays $50,000, suggest $50,000 to $60,000.

- If you believe the position pays $100,000, suggest $100,000 to $115,000.

- If you believe the position pays $200,000, suggest $200,000 to $225,000.

More specifically, if you conclude that the position pays approximately $100,000, your response to "What are you looking to make in your next opportunity?" should be something along the lines of this:

Based on the responsibilities of this position, I am looking to make between $100,000 and $115,000, plus bonus and equity (if available) that is commensurate with my peers. Is that within the range of this position?

I believe it is essential to start with "Based on the responsibilities of this position ..." because that is all the other person cares about — this position. Do not start with "What I want to make is ..." or "What I am looking for is ..." or "I am currently at $100,000, so I'm looking for $110,000."

The interviewer doesn't care because it isn't relevant. However, "Based on the responsibilities of this position ..." is indeed relevant to the conversation.

If the response to your question about the appropriateness of the range is "Yes," all you need to respond with is, "Great. Thank you." If the interviewer responds that your range is high, you can follow up with, "I am still very interested in the position; what is the range?" Unless the answer is completely unacceptable, make sure you communicate that you are still very interested in the position.

The objective is to keep the discussion moving forward to get an offer. This demonstrates that you want to have a discussion about compensation and that the discussion is not a one-way street. This also provides you with the information you need to form a decision. This way, you are in control of the process, not the employer.

If you are asked, "How much are you currently making?", assuming you currently make $100,000 with a 10% bonus, your answer should be, "I am currently making $100,000 with a 10% bonus; is that within your range?"

If the response is "Yes," say, "Great. Thank you."

If the response is that your current compensation is a little high, you can say, "I am still very interested in the position; what is the range?" Again, unless the answer is completely unacceptable, communicate that you are still very interested in the position.

If you are considering a position that involves a decrease either in compensation or title, the proper phrase can make all the difference. The interviewer is probing to discern if you are comfortable with either lower compensation or a reduced title.

Assuming you make $100,000 and the new position pays $90,000 or you are currently at a vice president level and the position for which you are interviewing is at a more junior level, an appropriate answer would be, "I am willing to take a step back as long as I see a path forward, and I do with this opportunity."

This assumes, of course, that you are comfortable with this strategy. Unless something is completely unacceptable to you, the object of the game is to get the offer. You get to decide whether to accept the offer, reject the offer, or negotiate more favorable terms, but without an offer, you do not have any options.

In summary, you need to be prepared, in advance, for the three responses the interviewer might give once you ask if your desired salary is within range. The interviewer can reply, "Yes, it is" ["Great!"], "You are a little high" ["That's fine; I am still very interested and would like to continue the discussion"], or "You are very high" ["I am willing to take a step back as long as I see a path forward, and I do with this situation"].

Preparation, as always, is key to your success.

Key Question to Ask Early in the Interview

As early as possible in the interview process, learn how the interviewer defines success. Determining this brings together two of the key elements of an effective job search. The first is to make no assumptions, and the second is to know your own background, both of which are discussed earlier in the book.

To recap, you may *think* you know why you are on an interview, but you really do not know. Recall the slide from Chapter Four about jumping to conclusions. Perhaps someone noticed something on your résumé that would fill a current gap in their organization or perhaps they liked your technical expertise. You need to find out exactly why you are on this interview. Only then will you be able to address the interviewer's concerns and demonstrate why you are the right person for the job.

You likewise need to know your own background so that you can hit the target you are trying to reach.

The reason you have prepared short stories for each of your attributes and strengths and for every bullet point on your résumé is so that when you learn why you are on the interview, you can bring forth your most relevant experiences to address the situation.

Assuming the interview is a big target, your job is to find the bull's eye. Otherwise, you're shooting blind and guessing. You find the bull's eye by asking the interviewer this key question:

> *Tell me, Mr. Jones, in the first six months to a year with this company, what would I need to accomplish for you to tell me I've done an outstanding job?* (Depending on the level of the position, it may be more appropriate to rephrase the time frame to three to six months rather than six months to a year.)

It is critical to ask this question early in the interview, because once you know the answer, you know what the interviewer is looking for. This sets the agenda for the rest of the interview. Because you know your background so thoroughly, you should have no problem following up on the interviewer's answer. With your best stories in hand, you can tailor your response and provide supporting examples from your background to fit the job requirements and address any concerns. For example, you might say, *"That is great, because at XYZ Company, I did just that by ..."*

In addition, up to this point, you probably have not said a great deal. Now you have the opportunity to focus the majority of your comments around how the interviewer answers this key question. Remember, no one cares why this is a good job opportunity for you. They care about how you can solve *their* problems and make a significant contribution to their team!

Ask this critical question of each and every person with whom you interview, not just the hiring manager, because everyone you talk with has a vote regarding whether to hire you. Each interviewer's answer will help to broadly define his or her overall concerns. It is then up to you to effectively address these concerns.

For example, if the interviewer responds with a highly technical concern that they would like to see handled, you know the direction the rest of the interview will take. If the response revolves around leadership, teamwork, or managerial skills or driving revenue, cost cutting, or growth, the hot button is in a different area. Regardless of what it is, or how it varies from person to person, you need to address each person's concern in order to convey that you are the best candidate for the job.

Do not save this question for the end of the interview. Identifying the person's concerns early allows you to focus your answers around those concerns and improve your chances for success. By the end of the interview, the interviewer has already determined whether or not you are moving forward and at that point, it is too late to make a difference. Asking this question now will not move the needle from "No" to "Yes."

Interview Flow

Interviews tend to flow in a fairly predictable fashion. A typical interview goes something like this:

- Someone (either the interviewer or a greeter) comes and gets you from the lobby. No matter who it is, immediately make eye contact and extend your hand.

- If this is the person you will be interviewing with, after some initial small talk, give your enthusiasm statement. (Remember, each person with whom you interview should be given this statement.)

- The interviewer will usually ask you to "Tell me about yourself" or "Take me through your résumé." You should be able to do this in a high-level fashion in forty-five to sixty seconds. Remember to spend the majority of your time on either your most current position or the one that best relates to the open position, bring in third party validation when possible, and do your best to present your summary in the "SAR" format of **S**ituation, **A**ction, and **R**esult so that you can give more than just the facts. (It is a bit useless to just repeat facts or bullet points, because the interviewer can read these off your résumé!)

- Next, the interviewer will most likely review the position description, which you made every effort to get a copy of prior to the interview. This is usually your opportunity to say, "Thank you very much for reviewing the position. I have a quick question: what would I need to accomplish in the first six months to a year for you to tell me that I've done an outstanding job?" Depending on how the interviewer answers this question, you present your experiences and proceed with the remainder of the interview.

- The balance of questions should follow the theme of how the interviewer answered the question above. Some behavioral questions may arise along with situational questions.

- Finally, the interview concludes. Because the "close" is so important, I discuss this in its own section at the end of the chapter.

Bring a Prop?

Using a prop is a judgment call. If you like, you can bring an example of prior work (as long as the information has been modified, redacted, or is not confidential) or a relevant paper you wrote in school.

When I was interviewing, I brought along a copy of a well-written five-page report that was developed for a former CFO. If appropriate, I would show the report to the CFO who was interviewing me as an example of my work, and it was always very well received.

If you decide to bring a prop, make sure it is small (no three-ring binders, please) and that it fits in your portfolio. Also, this prop is not to be given to the interviewer to keep but is rather an example of your work. Do not leave it behind.

Sell Yourself

Once, during a mock interview, it was pointed out to me that I came across as if I were evaluating and assessing the situation rather than being fully engaged and attentive to the interviewer's issues and concerns.

Avoid this. Instead, make an effort to identify the concerns of the interviewer and sell yourself rather than spending this time evaluating the interviewer, the position, or the company. If you are evaluating, it will show on your face and in your body language, so evaluate *after* the interview. You are on the interview to sell yourself and get an offer.

Go into the interview convicted, not hesitant and unsure. That is why you developed your playbook — to alleviate a good portion of the uncertainty. Believe it or not, when I was interviewing candidates as a hiring manager, individuals would occasionally tell me, "I think this is something I'm interested in."

Really? Clearly, those individuals did not move forward in the process.

The playbook allows you to choose your words prior to the interview, so mindfully eliminate words or phrases such as "I think." If you must use a quali-fier, use "I believe." Be convicted in your answers.

Additional Interviewing Tips

First, draw as many similarities as possible between your experience and the job you are interviewing for.

Second, know what you are looking for so that if you are asked what you are looking for in your next job, you will be able to answer. Craft this response to be high level rather than detailed. You do not have all of the information regarding a particular position, and you do not want to inadvertently put yourself in a box. Know what is important to you, but keep it general and relevant.

For example, you might say, "*I am looking for a position where my finance and leadership skills will have the greatest impact on the company by providing either the CFO, CEO, or business unit head with actionable financial information.*"

As discussed, company-supplied job descriptions are an excellent source of information for a response to this question. Find three or four position summaries that are of interest to you and incorporate relevant duties or requirements in your answer to this question.

Likewise, if you are asked, "Why are you interested in this company?", make sure you have three reasons at your fingertips. Examples might be:

- "I am very impressed with senior management."

- "I listened to the last earnings call (public companies only) and am impressed by the new direction of the company."

- "I believe I have the knowledge, skills, and ability to make a significant contribution to the team and believe it's a great mutual fit."

The same goes for, "What do you know about our company?" Use the information you gathered during your due diligence to put together three things you learned about the company or the interviewer. Be prepared to ask questions and to demonstrate that you have done some research. Do not be the person who goes to the networking meeting or interview not having bothered to do any research. This is cause for immediate elimination, and no doubt that is what will promptly happen.

Also be prepared for your interviewer to ask how your job search process is going and what other opportunities you might have in the works. The interviewer is attempting to determine if you are upbeat and positive about your search. Your response will indicate how you face adversity or professional challenges and how this may translate to your attitude on the job.

In addition to judging your attitude, this is a way for the interviewer to determine if others find you professionally attractive. Human nature is such that if others do not find you professionally attractive, the interviewer may not want to hire you either. Conversely, if others are interested in you, the interviewer is more likely to be interested as well.

To provide a strong answer to this question, be prepared to discuss, at a high level, three legitimate opportunities you are currently exploring. If you do not have three, you'd better get busy. For each of these opportunities, give the interviewer the following information:

- The round you are in (first, second, or third round of interviews) for the opportunity

- The position (V.P. of finance, director of planning, and so on) you are applying for

- The industry (healthcare, financial services, etc.)

This is short and to the point; you simply give the round, the position, and the industry. For example, if you are asked how your search is going, you might answer with, *"I'm in the third round with a financial services company for a VP of finance, the second round with a loyalty marketing company for a senior VP of planning role, and the first round with a healthcare provider for a VP forecasting position."*

If you are behind in your search, an effective approach would be to apply for positions you have sourced online. That way, you can honestly say you are in the first round for a legitimate position, because once you apply, you are in the first round.

Close Strong

A good ending is just as important as a good beginning, but most candidates do not know how to close an interview, which can create awkwardness. Often, when it becomes apparent that the interview is drawing to a close, many candidates mumble a quick "Thank you," offer a handshake, and hurry out the door. Instead of this bumbling conclusion, be prepared to close the interview the same way you started it, in a strong, enthusiastic, professional manner.

As with the rest of your preparation, script out your close and memorize it so that you know exactly what you are going to say. To effectively conclude the interview, use a slightly modified version of your enthusiasm statement that leaves a good final impression. It could go something like this:

> *Mr. Jones, I just wanted you to know that I was very interested in this position before we spoke. Now, after meeting with you, I am even more excited about the opportunity, particularly as it relates to [name the two things from the job description that genuinely excite you]. I believe I have the knowledge, skills, and ability to make a significant contribution to your team. I look forward to the next steps in the process.*

Or you might say:

> *I believe my background is a great fit for the position and that I can make a significant contribution to the team. I'm very excited about the opportunity and look forward to the next steps in the process.*

I am not a fan of the "soft close" during the interview. A soft close entails asking something such as, "Ms. Smith, do you know of any reason that I would not be asked to move forward in the process?"

I have always found such questions annoying and off-putting. Besides, I do not believe you can overcome someone's objection at this stage in the interview.

Instead, as with every other aspect of searching for and landing a job, thoroughly prepare for a strong and meaningful close.

CHAPTER SIX

Manage Phone Calls and Phone Interviews

It is very common for a first interview to consist of a "phone screen." This is typically conducted by a person in HR whose job it is to quickly determine if the candidate is a "fit" for the company and if compensation is an issue. These are usually fairly short calls, often twenty to thirty minutes long. This initial phone screen differs from the in-person interview in that you do not have a lot of time to make your points. For this reason, you need to be especially tight and concise in your answers, only thirty to forty seconds in duration. Being well prepared with succinct compact answers is the key to a successful phone interview.

Taking the Call

When is the best time to engage in a phone interview? Not when the interviewer calls unexpectedly. This isn't because you are playing hard to get. It's because you are unprepared for this very important conversation.

The interviewer is prepared with your résumé, your profile, the job description, and questions to ask. You, on the other hand, may be driving, cooking, or doing something totally unrelated to the interview when the call comes in. As a result, you are at a huge disadvantage mentally and perhaps physically.

Likewise, you do not want to take an unexpected phone call from a recruiter or interviewer who mentions that your background is intriguing and asks if you have a few minutes. In your excitement, you will probably say yes, and then you will be asked to talk about yourself. After several seconds of silence, you will blurt out an answer, but not as you had prepared it.

How do I know this? This disastrous scenario happened to me, and I don't want you to make the same mistake. Fortunately, by taking a few simple steps, you can shift the odds in your favor for a successful phone call or phone interview.

When such a call comes in, you have two choices — let it go to voice mail or answer it. I recommend letting it go to voice mail.

If you do decide to take the call, do not engage in an interview-type conversation. Rather, let the caller know that now is not a good time but that you are very interested in speaking to him or her, and would it be possible to talk at a different and mutually convenient time?

This allows you to conduct the call on your terms.

In my current business, Eureka Professional Services, I very rarely take a call from a number I do not recognize. If it is a prospect, he or she is prepared. I prefer to let the call go to voice mail, listen to the message, determine why the individual is calling, and perhaps learn who made the referral. This allows me to prepare for the phone call and, in turn, have a more meaningful conversation that best serves the prospect.

Determining Why You Received a Call

The most important question you can ask the caller, whether this individual is calling you cold or because of a résumé you sent in, is this:

What was it in my background that caught your interest?

This is critical information that allows you to better prepare for the interview. Ask this question even if you are going to call this individual back. The conversation can be as simple as this:

Interviewer: *Hi Jay. I just received your résumé and believe that you might be a great fit for this position. Do you have a few minutes?*

Response: *Thank you very much for calling. I'm very excited about this opportunity, but I'm driving right now. Can I call you back at 3:00?*

Interviewer: *Sure, that sounds great.*

Response: *Very good, I will call you then. I just have a quick question though: what was it about my background that caught your interest?*

The answer is critical to a successful next conversation and will immediately tell you what in your background to focus on during the interview. Remember that *Brain Games* slide? Don't make any assumptions about why the interviewer called! Most people bring several skills or areas of expertise to the table. By asking this key question, you will learn specifically what is important to the interviewer as well as what skills you possess that may help this individual solve his problem. You then need to stress those skills during the interview. If you do not ask this simple question, you are making assumptions and have only a general idea of why you were called.

Preparing for the Phone Interview

Proper preparation before any phone interview gives you a distinct advantage. In advance, please understand that a phone interview is very different from an in-person interview. When speaking on the phone, you are not able to pick up on visual clues like body language and facial expressions. Thus, your interview approach and preparation need to be different. The following tips can make your interview more comfortable and effective:

- Make sure you have a quiet place where you can carry on a conversation without distractions. This means closing the door to the room, turning off any radios, music, or TVs, and putting pets outside or giving them a treat to keep them occupied. In other words, no barking dogs or crying babies allowed! The interviewer or hiring authority needs and deserves your undivided attention.

- Along the same lines, do not chew gum, suck on hard candy, drink something with ice in it, or smoke, as these will make enough noise to be heard.

- Organize your playbook, résumé, job description, and any other notes you need in front of you. Spread them out in logical order so you can easily and quickly refer to them. You do not want to be shuffling papers or clicking on a keyboard while trying to talk.

- Have the interviewer's LinkedIn profile printed off or up on your computer screen to refresh your memory as to the caller's background.

- Remind yourself to speak in sound bites of thirty to forty seconds each. Use the stopwatch on your smart phone if necessary. Be concise and tight in your answers, and do not ramble. Attention spans are much shorter on the phone than in person, and you do not want to lose your audience.

You may even wish to dress for the phone interview as if you were conducting the interview in person. This is a purely personal preference, but dressing the part may give you a psychological edge. In addition, you may wish to determine if your voice sounds different or better when you are seated and talking on the phone versus when you stand and talk on the phone. Practice different scenarios, determine the conditions that work best for you, and craft them accordingly to increase your chances of success.

CHAPTER SEVEN

Special Advice for Special Groups

Different groups of people have different preparation and interviewing needs and concerns. A few of these special interest groups are addressed next.

For College Students

Many studies highlight the challenges employers today face in finding qualified job candidates among college graduates. The areas of concern include basic personal effectiveness competencies such as:

- Creativity

- Willingness to learn

- Ability to learn quickly

- Adaptability

- Work ethic

- Discipline

- Critical thinking skills

- Interpersonal skills

- Ability to collaborate as part of a team

If you are a college student, I challenge you to quell these concerns. Do so by addressing them in your playbook and making sure you demonstrate these quality traits and characteristics positively during an interview.

For Veterans

If you are a veteran, you learned many valuable skills in the military that are transferable to the business world. The challenge is often in communicating them effectively to those in the private sector, using the language of business rather than military jargon, which may be unfamiliar and foreign to them.

Keep in mind that people generally like to hire candidates with whom they have things in common. When candidates use language specific to their industry, military or otherwise, they may be communicating to the other person how different they are rather than how similar.

Take a few minutes to think about the functions you performed and the skills you acquired during your service. Below are some key words and phrases you might use when drafting your résumé or bio to help articulate transferable skills. These words, along with key words from the company-supplied description of the position you are applying for, can go under the "Summary of Qualifications" in your résumé and under "Competencies" in your bio. They will help convey the message that you are very skilled and more similar to business people than different from them.

Key Words and Phrases for Veterans

- Results focused

- Strategic planning

- Inspire others

- Motivator

- Ability to lead

- Skilled in conflict resolution

- Analyze and summarize complex data into useful information

- Develop succession planning

- Develop policies and procedures

- Supervise and train

- Increase morale

- Think strategically

- Solve complex problems

- Respond under pressure

- Excellent organizational skills

- Empower others

- Analyze and develop an operations plan

- Develop and implement systems

- Create value

- Creative thinker

- Positive mindset and attitude

- Drive and determination

- Design training programs

- Customer service oriented

- Work well under pressure

- Never quits

Finally, for each key word or phrase that you use, remember to create a twenty- to thirty-second story demonstrating proficiency in that skill in case you are asked to elaborate.

For Older Workers

I am often asked if age is an issue when applying for a position. The answer is usually yes, but since you can't do anything about it, you might as well address it head on.

Employers cannot directly ask about your age. What they can ask is, "What are your long-term goals?" This is a subtle way of determining whether you are going to retire in a few years and waste all their training!

The proper way to address this question is to answer with a reference to long-term career goals. For example, say something like:

> *My long-term career goals are to be in a position of increasing responsibility where I can continue to make a significant contribution to the organization.*

The key here is to focus on what you can do for the organization and to emphasize that you are looking to add value to the team. Also convey that you intend to work long enough so that the company will receive a healthy payback on the investment they are making in hiring and training you.

For Those Who Have Been Out of the Workforce for a While

If you have been out of the workforce for more than six months, you may be asked to explain what you have been doing during this time. The hiring authority or

HR person wants to know whether your work skills are current and what you have done to keep up your abilities. Have you been taking courses to enhance your education? Acquiring new talents to add to your list?

Focus on the positives of the time you have spent in transition. Even if you have been unable to work, communicate the efforts you have made to stay in touch with others in the field. Online courses, seminars, and staying connected with other professionals all have their benefits.

Perhaps you have been raising a family or recovering from a long-term illness. Perhaps you have been exploring a different job path entirely. As needed, reconnect or make new connections. Search out professional organizations or support groups specific to your career path. Professional organizations often come with job leads that are only available through membership. Networking with others in your specific field can also provide you with a list of training options to enhance your résumé.

A Word about Tax Deductions

While you are in transition and job hunting, some of the expenses you incur may be tax deductible. There are strict limitations as to what can be deducted, so familiarize yourself with the rules before filing your taxes. In order to deduct job search expenses, you must meet the following criteria:

- The expenses for your job search must be in your current field.

- The expenses are not deductible if your employer or another party reimburses you for them.

- Employment and job placement agency fees may be deducted while you are searching for a job.

- The cost of preparing and mailing copies of your résumé to prospective employers is deductible.

- If you must travel to look for a new job, you may be able to deduct your travel expenses.

- Job search expenses are usually filed as a miscellaneous itemized deduction; to be deductible, your total miscellaneous deductions must exceed two percent (2%) of your adjusted gross income.

- You cannot deduct job search expenses if you have a long break between the end of your last job and the time you start looking for a new one.

- First-time employees cannot deduct job search expenses.

These tips aside, I am not a tax accountant, and tax laws are constantly changing. You can find additional up-to-date information at http://www.irs.gov. Look for Publication 529, Miscellaneous Deductions, an IRS booklet that is available on IRS.gov or by calling 800-TAX-FORM (800-829-3676).

Final Tips

Whoever you are and whatever your background, the job search entails many things beyond your control. These include having someone return your call, getting an interview for a seemingly perfect job, and receiving an offer. You must not dwell on the things that are out of your control.

Instead, to improve your peace of mind and overall sanity, focus on the things you *can* control. At least five things are within your control in every job search:

1. Your attitude

2. The amount of preparation you do

3. Your body language

4. The way you dress

5. The way you want to be introduced

You should also be able to articulate what's important to you in the context of your career just in case you are asked. This might include responses you include in your playbook such as:

- I want my work to have meaning.

- I want to be able to make an impact on the company or my department.

- I want to make a difference.

Knowing who you are, what you want, and how to meet the expectations of those you will be meeting are, happily, very much within your control.

PART III

The Job Offer

Congratulations! Your thoughtful preparation has paid off, and you are about to receive a job offer.

Properly accepting the offer keeps all the goodwill and positive momentum that built up during the hiring process going into the initial days on the new job. Likewise, understanding how to properly negotiate the offer will keep both you and your new boss happy as you embark on your next career.

By the same token, bungling either of these components can taint what could otherwise be a very positive experience.

Once again, preparation and practice will pay off in this most important aspect of securing a new job.

CHAPTER EIGHT

Accepting the Offer

Think for a moment about why you are receiving an offer. In addition to being technically competent and having the right chemistry, you received an offer because you were well prepared and enthusiastic about joining the company. That same preparation and enthusiasm needs to be applied during the acceptance and negotiation process.

It is important to think about what you require to take the job *before* the offer comes in. At the time an offer is extended is not the right time to begin considering what you want or need in your offer. Think through your options and bottom line prior to receiving the offer. Once you know what you need in order to accept the job, write out what you want to say in your playbook.

How *Not* to Accept a Job Offer

The following is a sure-fire way to get off to a poor start with a prospective new employer:

> *"Well, this is a decent offer but I was hoping for more money ... I'll accept it anyway."*

If I were the hiring manager and this was the lukewarm response I received after extending the offer, I would second-guess my decision.

How to Accept a Job Offer

On the other hand, the following responses are gracious and appropriate and will be received in kind:

> *"Thank you very much, Ms. Smith! I am very excited about the opportunity to work for XYZ Company, and I really like what I have seen."*

or

> *"This is a very fair offer; I accept, and I look forward to joining the team!"*

These responses are well crafted and will make the hiring authority feel good about bringing you on board.

How to Ask for Time to Consider a Job Offer

I do not advocate deferring an acceptance simply to play hard to get. It does not advance your position in the least. However, if you need to consider an offer — which is perfectly acceptable — you can say something along the lines of:

> *My intent is to accept, but I would like until the end of the day to review the offer.*

or

> *My intent is to accept, but I would like to discuss it with my husband/wife and get back to you by 3:00 tomorrow.*

If you give a specific time, be sure to get back in touch when you said you would. The key is to be upbeat and excited and to use the phrase "my intent is to accept," assuming, of course, that you are very interested in the position. By being enthusiastic, you are also building an advocate in the event that you do want to negotiate the offer further. Remember, the person you are talking with is now, in effect, your agent in any negotiations to come. You need this individual on your side.

How to Reject a Job Offer

If your intent is to reject an offer, handle the situation with professionalism and grace. There is no need to go into great detail regarding your decision. Say something concise such as:

> *Thank you for the opportunity to meet with everyone and learn about the position. However, at this point, I believe it is in my best interests to pursue another opportunity.*

How to React to a Rejection

If you do not receive a job offer after what you thought was a good interview, it could simply be a matter of chemistry. No matter how qualified you may be for a position and no matter how prepared you are for an interview, not everyone will like you or consider you the optimal fit.

You have to move on and not dwell on the rejection. If you went through a recruiter, you might be able to get some useful feedback, but this is rare and usually does not occur. Nobody enjoys delivering unflattering news, so rather than report that you were not a fit to you or a recruiter, you will often receive a rejection reason that cannot be fixed.

It is common for employers to notify candidates by email if they don't make the initial cut for a first interview, but once the interview process begins, most companies will call to let candidates know if they are not moving forward in the process. That said, if you are applying to a "blind" ad (where no company name is given), it is common for companies to ignore candidates whom they have decided not to interview.

Typical reasons for not moving forward include the lack of a desired degree such as a CPA or MBA from a top 10 school, insufficient direct industry experience, or the dreaded "I'm sorry, but you are over qualified." These negatives cannot be easily fixed.

The truth is, most individuals simply want you to quietly go away. They have made their choice and want to move on. You should do the same, but continue to act professionally and think long-term. You never know when you might have another shot at this company or run into these individuals again. Say something like this:

> *Thank you for the opportunity to interview with* [name the company]. *If any other positions become available that you believe I might be a fit for, I would be very interested in returning to speak with you again.*

I have had clients receive rejections because they lacked a skill or asset who, upon using this response, found themselves called back to interview for other positions within the organization.

CHAPTER NINE

Negotiating the Offer

L et's now build on the foundation that resulted in the offer being extended to you. Because you formulated and executed your playbook, you were well prepared throughout the interview process. You also demonstrated appropriate enthusiasm. You were likewise respectful and your answers were succinct and relevant.

You now need to apply those same standards and practices to the negotiation process. There are two things to remember when negotiating. First, everything (within reason) is negotiable. Second, it is more about how you ask for what you want than *what* you ask for.

What Can Be Negotiated?

Components of the job offer to consider and possibly negotiate include the following:

- Base compensation

- Title

- Job grade

- Bonus

- Equity

- Vacation or paid time off

If the company offers other benefits, make sure you understand what they are, how they work, and when you are eligible to receive them. You want to understand the company's:

- 401(k) or 403(b) matching policy

- Medical plan

- Vacation policy or paid time off

- Employee stock purchase program (if applicable)

Keep in mind that the person who extended the offer, whether it was HR or your new boss, may not have the authority to approve changes without first seeking approval from others. However, you want and need this person to be an advocate for you because this is who will represent you to those who do have the authority to make changes.

This authority is going to want to know what your attitude and response were to the original offer. If your agent responds that you came across as disappointed and lackluster, you have greatly diminished your negotiating position.

When negotiating, it is in your best interests for your agent to report that your "intent is to accept" and that you are excited about the opportunity and looking forward to working with the company. This sets a positive tone. Your odds of effectively negotiating changes to the offer increase substantially, because the powers that be will be in a frame of mind to work with you and come to mutually beneficial terms.

When negotiating changes to your offer, assess what you consider to be the "must haves" versus the "nice to haves." What will you accept as minimum terms? What will cause you to be thrilled with accepting an offer? Be prepared for what you will accept. However, never, ever discuss need! The employer does not care about your personal circumstances, compensation, or paid time off needs. Whether you just bought a house, are recently married, or are expecting an addition to the family is not relevant, so do not bring any of it into the discussion.

Compensation

When negotiating compensation, as discussed in Chapter Five, it is best to not ask for specific dollars. Instead, use ranges, which give the employer some flexibility.

For example, if you are offered $100,000 but believe based on your research that the base should be $110,000, a good starting phrase could be this:

> *Based on the responsibilities of the position, I believe the compensation should be between $110,000–$115,000. Is it possible to bump up the salary to within that range?*

Also, getting creative and being flexible can be effective. Compensation can include many components, including base salary, signing bonus, annual bonus, and equity. All of these can be negotiated to arrive at a mutually satisfactory final compensation number.

For example, if you are offered a total compensation package of $115,000 (a $100,000 base and up to a 15% bonus) and you want $120,000, ask if the company can be creative and get your total compensation to $120,000 between base and bonus. Do your best to allow options between base, bonus, and signing bonus to get you where you want to be. Very specific requests can be more difficult for the company to deliver.

Title

If the issue is title, you may consider saying something like this:

> *I'm very excited about the opportunity, and the compensation is very fair. My intent is to accept. What I believe is very important, based on the responsibilities of the position, is that I come in at an SVP level rather than a VP.*

Then give a reason why, such as:

> *Given my position, I believe I will need this title to be effective in dealing with my peers [or whatever you believe the legitimate issue is].*

Other components of the job — job grade, bonus, equity, vacation or paid time off — can all be negotiated as well, but that brings me to another important point, which is to thoughtfully consider how many things you should actually negotiate.

How Many Things Should Be Negotiated?

As mentioned, prior to the offer being extended, it is important to determine exactly what you want. Assuming you do want to negotiate, be careful not to ask for too much. More specifically, I believe that asking for two changes to the original offer is sufficient. For example, total compensation and title, or title and paid time off.

In my opinion, asking for three changes comes off as greedy. This is a judgment call, but having been the hiring manager, if a candidate asks for too much, it sends a signal that usually isn't positive.

An exception to this is if you are at the senior executive level, where it is common to have very high compensation packages that contain multiple components, most of which are open for negotiation.

Managing Multiple Offers

If you are fortunate enough to have multiple offers or are waiting to hear from another company about an offer but the current company is pressing you for an answer, it is perfectly acceptable to ask for more time to consider the offer. An effective way to accomplish this is as follows:

> *Thank you very much, Ms. Smith. I'm very excited about the opportunity to work for XYZ Company. You are my first choice, and my intent is to accept. However, I have been talking with other companies, and I owe them the opportunity to present their offers. You are my first choice* [you can say it this second time to make the point], *but I would like to have* [name your time window] 24 [or 48] *hours to get back to you.*

At this point, you need to be prepared for Ms. Smith to attempt to close the deal by asking you what you need to consider. You can either present your concern, if you want to close the deal, or you can simply reiterate your excitement and interest and tell her you will call her back.

Also, please remember that whoever you are talking with is always your "first choice." After all, no one wants to be number two!

PART IV

Effective Onboarding

Congratulations on landing your new job! You may be "in," but even if you've negotiated your package and are all set to start, you're not yet "on," as in being effectively and fully onboarded.

Effective onboarding is critical for long-term success and personal satisfaction, so like every other aspect of getting a new job, you need to think it through and act accordingly.

CHAPTER TEN

Your First One Hundred Days

The first one hundred days on the new job are critical. Because early momentum sets the stage for your tenure with the company, it is in your best interests to play an active role during this "honeymoon" period. Critical steps to take right off the top include the following:

- Follow up on personal communication.

- Personalize your office.

- Schedule one-on-ones with your boss.

- Schedule one-on-ones with relevant peers and internal customers.

- Maintain your network and help others.

Remember, you are trying to understand the big picture, so look for low hanging fruit/quick wins and identify long-term improvements you can make. Also look for common themes when talking to people, as these will signal what you should perhaps be focusing on. You might also ask your staff for their top five ideas on improving either the department or their function. You might be amazed at what the people who are actually doing the work have to say about how to do it better!

Don't offer advice yet on how to fix anything; you simply don't know enough about the company, culture, roles, and processes.

To help you prepare for your first hundred days on the new job, I strongly recommend you read the excellent book for how to effectively onboard a company titled *The New Leader's 100-Day Action Plan: How to Take Charge, Build Your Team, and Get Immediate Results* by George B. Bradt, Jayme A. Check, and Jorge E. Pedraza. Some parts of the book are geared toward CEOs and others to people in sales and management, but a good portion of the book has broad appeal and is very beneficial to all new hires.

Follow Up on Personal Communication

After you land, I urge you to send a personal note to every person who helped you along the way. Those people want and deserve to know what happened and how your search ended.

A personalized handwritten note is ideal and an email is perfectly acceptable, though a mass distribution email should never be sent for these purposes. You need to take the time to individually acknowledge each person who helped you when you needed it most. The least you can do is send a simple, informative, personal email expressing your thanks. You never know when you may find yourself in need of additional help from these very kind people.

It may take several days to get these emails out, but it is simply the right thing to do. I met over ninety people when I was in transition, and I sent each person a personalized email upon landing my new position. I have had people tell me how much they appreciated me both closing the loop (telling them what happened) and expressing my thanks in a personal message.

Personalize Your Office

Bring in your personal belongings and set up your office/cubicle and make it your own, but not on "company time." Rather, do it either before or after hours or on the weekend. This might sound like a minor point, but I believe it makes a difference by sending an early message that you are serious about your new role and that you value company time.

Schedule One-on-Ones with Your Boss

I urge all my newly employed clients to schedule one-on-ones with their new bosses. Ask your boss/manager what works best with his or her schedule, i.e., once a week, twice a month, and so on.

In a conversation years ago, a well-respected CEO told me he had one-on-ones with his former boss every Friday afternoon. His boss was much more relaxed then, it was a relatively quiet time in the office, and his boss was generally more receptive to his ideas.

This makes sense. Think about the difference between meeting your manager at 9:00 a.m. Monday morning versus 4:00 p.m. Friday afternoon. You get the point. The timing can make for a much more effective meeting. For this reason, try to schedule these meetings on Friday afternoons. Not only are Fridays more casual in most companies, but Friday afternoons are often less hectic and the atmosphere more conducive to constructive conversation and feedback.

I recommend developing a one-page document outlining topical bullet points to cover at these weekly meetings. The top half of the page should highlight four to six items listing your accomplishments since your last meeting, while the bottom half (this is actually more important) lists four to six bullet points highlighting what you plan to accomplish by the next meeting.

This one-page high-level document will contain a great deal of white space, since each bullet will contain one, at most two, sentences. Filling out the top half with meaningful points might initially be difficult, but simple tasks such as "attended training" or "meeting with various key people" are part of your initial onboarding process.

The reason I consider the bottom half more important is that it allows you to discuss with your manager the specifics of what you should be working on and to get his or her feedback on that direction. This way, especially early on, you avoid wasting time on the wrong projects and you simultaneously give your manager the opportunity to provide corrective feedback early in the process. This is a great way to keep your goals aligned with those of your boss.

During these meetings, talk about gaining short-term key milestones and identify some "quick wins" to gain momentum and a positive reputation. In other words, unless your employer has already done so, take charge of the onboarding process.

Schedule One-on-Ones with Relevant Peers and Internal Customers

You should also plan on meeting with relevant peers and internal customers early on in your new job. When you meet with these key internal stakeholders, ask open-ended questions about their needs and listen carefully to what they say.

Do not offer advice (yet) on how to fix anything. At this stage, you do not know enough about the company's culture, key roles, and processes. Simply listen and gather information so that you can do a great job. Appropriate open-ended questions include the following:

- How can I improve the department?

- What do you believe I need to do to be successful?

- What is your biggest pain point?

Going into problem-solving mode at this early stage can be a huge turnoff to others, who might resent your attempt to solve on your third day what they've been trying to deal with for a decade. This is no way to win friends and influence people.

Of course, all of this assumes that you were not brought in to quickly clean house and make drastic changes!

As a gentle reminder, it is not generally expected that you transform the company in the first two weeks — take three!

Maintain Your Network and Help Others

Once you start your new job, it may be difficult to make time to network. However, during your job search, you spent a great deal of time and resources building a network, and you should continue to maintain it. Do not forget all those who helped you during your search. Make it a goal to spend an hour per week taking phone calls, meeting with people in your office, or taking a person in transition to lunch.

Your primary focus and energies should be spent on your new job, but you need to keep your network alive and well, whether that means attending professional organization meetings or having lunch with contacts. This is very important in the event that you choose to seek another opportunity or find yourself in transition once again. You do not want to have to start from scratch, and you do not want to be known as one of those people who only reaches out when in need.

Also, now is your opportunity to make all the difference in the world by providing much-needed hope to someone else in transition. Give back what was so freely given to you. You just might be able to offer advice and feedback and make some introductions that could lead to that person's next opportunity, so be willing to pay it forward!

In Conclusion

I am confident that when you put the skills and techniques outlined in this book into practice, you will not only be better prepared than the competition for both networking and interviewing but will also conduct a more efficient and effective job search. In turn, you will significantly shorten your search and land your next opportunity more quickly.

In the meantime, best wishes and good luck!

Jay D. Fusaro

www.eurekaprofessionalservices.com

jay.fusaro@sbcglobal.net

PART V

Exhibits

The exhibits that follow offer effective examples of the cover letter, the résumé, the bio, and the additional questions all job candidates should prepare.

Exhibit A: Cover Letter

Ms. Smith,

I am applying for the position of Vice President — Corporate Planning for XYZ Corporation. I have proven accomplishments in financial planning with multiple lines of business and identifying risks and opportunities within the forecast. I have led cross functional teams of up to twenty to solve company-wide problems.

When you read a summary of my qualifications, you will see that I meet the requirements of the position. I believe I can make a significant impact at XYZ Corporation.

The enclosed résumé summarizes my accomplishments, and I look forward to an interview. Thank you in advance for your consideration.

Best regards,

Jay D. Fusaro

Exhibit B: Résumé

J A Y D . F U S A R O , **C P A**

C (469) 223-5201 ▪ jay.fusaro@sbcglobal.net

S U M M A R Y O F Q U A L I F I C A T I O N S

- PLANNING AND ANALYSIS
- BUILDING CORPORATE INFRASTRUCTURE
- M&A DUE DILIGENCE

- BUDGETING AND FORECASTING
- ACQUISITION INTEGRATION
- IPO EXPERIENCE

- FINANCIAL MODELING
- POST-INTEGRATION FOLLOW-UP
- INTERNAL CONTROLS / SOX

- OPERATIONAL ANALYTICS
- PROJECT MANAGEMENT
- CAPEX EVALUATION

- MANAGEMENT REPORTING
- PRESENTATION SKILLS
- PROCESS IMPROVEMENTS

Highly accomplished, enterprising Top Finance Professional, who builds, directs, and motivates teams on complex projects. Communicates clear standards to ensure staff understanding of company goals. Identifies opportunities to reduce costs, realizing extensive gains in profitability. Forward-thinking leader, who lays the groundwork for lasting corporate success and profitability.

P R O F E S S I O N A L E X P E R I E N C E

MoneyGram International, Dallas, Texas (NYSE: MGI)   2011 – 2012
$1.3 billion publicly held company and a leader in global money transfer and bill payment services through a worldwide network of more than 284,000 agent locations in 196 countries.

Senior Director, Financial Planning
Managed teams of up to 47. Led the Global planning and forecasting efforts for the Americas, Europe, Middle East, Africa, and Asia Pacific. Prioritized $83 million of capital expenditures.

- Led financial planning and forecasting for 5 SG&A divisions, including foreign entities in EMEAAP and Latin America totaling $1.3 billion in revenue and $500 million in annual spend.

- Provided financial, analytical, and strategic planning information to the executive committee, which led to increased
  visibility and predictability in financial performance to support
  8% revenue growth and 17% CAGR.

- Defined an enterprise strategy for information management
  to support the company's needs and challenges for financial
  reporting. Standardized and streamlined company-wide
  reporting from disparate systems (Essbase and Cognos),
  resulting in more accurate and timely information.

- Delivered concise forecast summaries to the Chief Financial Officer as well as an action plan to close an $11.9
  million expense gap to plan. Oversaw the preparation of
  presentations for the Board of Directors and assisted with
  earnings release preparation.

Zale Corporation, Irving, Texas (NYSE: ZLC)   2010 – 2011
*$1.7 billion publicly held company and a leading retailer of fine
jewelry, operating over 1,930 retail locations throughout the
United States, Canada, and Puerto Rico.*

Vice President, Corporate Planning
Led financial planning, monthly forecasting, and capital
expenditures for company's six brands. Upgraded a team of
16. Co-chaired a team that identified annual run rate savings in
excess of $5 million.

- Directed initiative to implement three best-of-class performance management systems on time and on budget, which
  reduced forecasting cycles by 15%, improving the strategic
  decision-making process.

- Prioritized $30 million in capital expenditures for six brands,
  including identifying risks and opportunities.

- Led company's three- and five-year modeling for P&L, cash
  flow, and capital expenditures.

Alliance Data, Plano, Texas (NYSE: ADS)   1998 – 2010
*$3 billion publicly held Fortune 1000 company, is a leading
provider of loyalty and marketing solutions. Approximately 7,000
associates and over 50 locations worldwide.*

Vice President, Corporate Planning
Worked closely with Chief Financial Officer and Chief Executive

Officer. Led financial planning, monthly forecasting, and capital expenditures for company's three major lines of business.

- Established financial planning infrastructure, including staff development and controls, to manage growth in revenue from $300 million to more than $3 billion over ten years. Met or exceeded Wall Street earnings expectations for 35 consecutive quarters.
- Collaborated with a cross-functional team of company executives responsible for completing $180 million Initial Public Offering, providing analysis and support to executive committee and Board of Directors.
- Delivered CAGR of revenue 12%, EBITDA 15%, and EPS 18% by improving reliability and accuracy of company-wide forecast, enabling management to make informed decisions in a timely manner.
- Integrated eight acquisitions into company's financial platform and assisted in the divestiture of three lines of business, eliminating a cash-flow drain of $15 million.
- Delivered actionable financial information and analysis to CFO, based on updates to 12-month forecast, ensuring a focus on critical business issues by addressing risks and opportunities by line of business.
- Strengthened controls on $85 million of capital spending, including prioritizing requests and ROI analysis to maximize liquidity during times of extreme volatility in capital markets.
- Recruited, developed, and retained top-quality talent and built highly effective staff.
- Conducted periodic assessments of line of business financial performance. Provided recommendations and support for resolution of underlying business issues.

Comerica Bank, Dallas, Texas   1993 – 1998

Senior Vice President, Finance   (1997–1998)

Vice President, Management Accounting and Planning (1993–1997)

- Delivered financial and strategic planning information to executives and business unit managers of Texas and

California divisions, with $4 billion in total assets and $500 million in revenue.

- Upgraded and managed staff of 11 professionals in two states.
- Designed and implemented comprehensive monthly forecasting process for two lines of business.

Bank One, Dallas, Texas   1991 – 1993

Assistant Vice President, Management Reporting

- Led business planning process as well as monthly forecast for the Texas bank and provided senior-level financial expertise to Senior Vice President of Corporate Planning and the state Chief Financial Officer.

ADDITIONAL EXPERIENCE

John Hancock Financial Services, Boston, Massachusetts, **Senior Management Consultant,** 1989–1991. Provided business consulting for several divisions. Improved processes, reduced cycle times, and reduced costs.

Bank of New England, Boston, Massachusetts, **Banking Officer,** 1986–1989. Developed corporate-wide profitability reports for this $30 billion bank spanning four states.

RTC Systems, Attleboro, Massachusetts, **Corporate Accountant,** 1983–1986. Developed and implemented an accounting system for company in start-up environment with annual sales of $50 million.

EDUCATION AND CERTIFICATIONS

Northeastern University, Boston, Massachusetts, **Bachelor of Science, Business Administration**

President, Boston Student Affiliation of the National Association of Accountants

President, Northeastern University Accounting Society

Certified Public Accountant, Texas

AFFILIATIONS

American Institute of Certified Public Accountants

Financial Executives International, Dallas Chapter

Sammons Center for the Arts; Past Board Member, Compensation and Audit Committee

Art Centre of Plano, Plano Texas; Past Treasurer, Board Member

Exhibit C: Bio

Jay Fusaro, CPA: Financial Professional

(469) 223-5201 ; Jay.Fusaro@sbcglobal.net

Competencies

Team Leadership
- Builds and leads high performing teams
- Communicates clear standards
- Creates vision
- Ability to motivate and challenge
- Strong, persuasive leadership skills

Analytical Thinking
- Intuitive thinker
- Generates ideas
- Creative problem solver
- Financially "savvy"

Relationship Building
- Builds credibility and trust
- Delivers results
- Collaborative operational manager
- Participative management style

Develops Others
- Mentors and coaches staff
- Direct but diplomatic
- Lead by example
- Values an open exchange of ideas when gathering information

Character
- Highest personal and professional integrity
- Ability to earn the trust of co-workers
- Sensitivity and tact in stressful situations
- High energy, flexible under pressure
- Difference maker

Professional Achievements
- Led financial planning and forecasting for 5 SG&A , including foreign entities totaling $1.3 billion in revenue and $500 million in annual spend
- Exceeded Wall Street earnings expectations for 35 consecutive quarters
- Managed revenue growth from $300 million to $3 billion
- Provided earnings visibility and predictability as well as input to earnings guidance
- Delivered CAGR of revenue 12%, EBITDA 15%, EPS 18% on a consistent basis by improving the reliability and accuracy of the company-wide forecast
- Provided M&A integration, converted 8 acquisitions and 3 divestitures, eliminating a cash flow drain of $15 million
- Led 3 diverse cross-functional teams
- Interpreted complex financial and strategic issues and translated them into actionable choices for executive teams
- Interfaced closely with CEO and CFO as the financial planning expert

Areas of Expertise
- Building and developing high-performing teams
- Recruiting, developing, and mentoring top talent
- Financial planning and future-looking strategy, while achieving day-to-day results
- Excellent presentation skills

Professional Biography
- Money Gram International
- Zale Corporation
- Alliance Data
- Comerica Bank

Target Functions
- VP Financial Planning
- VP Finance
- CFO, small to mid-size company

Target Companies
- Frito-Lay / PepsiCo
- Dean Foods
- Pizza Hut
- DrPepper Snapple Group
- e-Rewards
- Thomson Reuters
- Pegasus Solutions
- Concentra
- Fiserv
- Access Pharmaceuticals
- Neiman Marcus
- Kimberly-Clark
- Cinemark
- Safety Kleen Systems
- 7-Eleven

Exhibit D: Additional Questions to Prep

In addition to the questions listed in Chapter Three, you should prepare to answer a number of additional questions typically asked in the job interview process. These questions are as applicable to interns and college graduates entering the workforce as they are to veterans and seasoned employees.

Many firms use these questions because they provide a clearer picture of each candidate and also give an indication of how that person would work in either a team setting or on his or her own.

As with every other aspect of the job search, the answers require a good deal of thought, consideration, and practice to keep from sounding rehearsed, but the time you spend mastering this list will pay off when the big moment — the interview — comes.

- What accomplishments are you most proud of?

- What challenges have you faced in the past two years and how did you overcome them?

- Give an example of how you successfully dealt with someone who was difficult.

- Give an example of how one of your strengths has benefitted you when working in a team environment.

- Why do you want to work at this firm? (This can also be worded as "What do you know about our company?")

- Why are you interested in this particular division/area of the firm?

- Tell me about a time you failed.

- Give an example of a time you succeeded.

- What's the most difficult thing you've ever had to do?

- Give examples of how well you work under pressure.

- What are you looking to get out of a job (or internship) with this firm? (This can also be worded as "What are you looking for in your next job?")

- What are ways you have provided quality in a work assignment? How would you deal with the demands for quality in a fast-paced position where you don't have the luxury of time?

- Tell me about yourself. (Remember your sixty-second biography.)

- How would you describe your leadership skills?

- Give a situation in your past work (or school) experience where you demonstrated problem-solving skills.

- Where do you see yourself in five years? Ten years?

- Tell me about a time when you had an idea but your team was not willing to accept it. How did you go about presenting this idea and trying to persuade them to accept it?

- What did you learn from your last job (or internship)?

- Describe some situations where you've had to use business or technical writing skills.

- What makes you stand out from other candidates?

ABOUT THE AUTHORS

Jay D. Fusaro is the principal and founder of Eureka Professional Services where, as an interview coach, he provides his clients with the skills and techniques necessary to successfully conduct efficient and effective job searches. On average, Jay's clients experience a 65% interview success rate and many clients receive multiple offers, often for a greater compensation level than they were anticipating.

Jay is a CPA in the state of Texas and a graduate of Northeastern University in Boston, Massachusetts. He earned a Business Coaching Certificate from the Learning Resources Network in partnership with Southern Methodist University. He was Vice President of Financial Planning for Alliance Data during its successful IPO and has both built and led high-performing teams throughout his career, as well as implementing highly effective internal mentoring programs.

Jay's career encompasses $50 million start-ups to

$3 billion public companies. He has extensive experience in financial services where, among other positions, he served as Senior Vice President of Finance for Comerica Bank Texas. He has been a guest speaker at the Texas Society of CPA's Expo Conferences in Houston, San Antonio, and Arlington.

As part of Jay's continued effort to give back to the community, he conducts seminars at the Dallas Veterans Administration, at local churches, and at various business organizations that focus on outplacement as well as non-profits that are dedicated to women's causes. He is a current member of both the American Institute of Certified Public Accountants and the Texas Society of Certified Public Accountants. He is a past member of Financial Executives International, Dallas chapter, past board member of the Sammons Center for the Arts where he served on both the compensation and audit committees, and past treasurer and board member of the Art Centre of Plano in Plano, Texas.

Jay currently resides in Eureka Springs, Arkansas, with his wife Rosemary after living in the Dallas, Texas, area for twenty-four years.

Rosemary Davis Fusaro was a Dallas banker for more than twenty-five years and spent most of her career focusing on privately held businesses and their owners. Prior to her retirement in 2014, she was the Executive Vice President/Chief Lending Officer for the state-chartered Liberty Capital Bank based in Addison, Texas. Liberty Capital Bank opened its doors in September of 2008 with $10 million and grew to more than $130 million in assets during her tenure.

Immediately prior to joining Liberty Capital Bank, Rosemary served as Senior Vice President of Comerica Bank, where she was a senior originator and assistant group manager of a regional office. Her career in the Dallas financial services market also includes serving as Senior Vice President of Compass Bank and Bank of America Business Credit (Fleet Capital Corp.).

Rosemary holds a BA in economics from Douglass College, Rutgers University, and an MBA in finance from the Stern School of Business, New York University. She began her commercial lending career with Citicorp's healthcare commercial lending department in Dallas in 1989. Her first job out of college was with Bear Stearns & Co.'s Mergers and Acquisitions Group in New York City.

Rosemary served on the board of directors of The Family Place, where she was active on the finance committee. She also served on the board of trustees of CREW in the Community, the philanthropic arm of CREW (Commercial Real Estate Women), Dallas.

While a member of CREW, she also served on several committees and was the chair of the sponsor committee.

She is a past president of the Dallas/Fort Worth chapter of the Association for Corporate Growth and served as secretary-treasurer of the Commercial Finance Association's Southwest chapter. In 2013, Rosemary was honored by *Addison Magazine* with their Top Female Executive award.